MICROBITES
FLIGHT
RIVETING READS FOR CURIOUS KIDS

MICROBITES
FLIGHT
RIVETING READS FOR CURIOUS KIDS

By
Reg Grant

Consultant
Michael Allaby

Second Edition

DK London

Senior Editor Sam Atkinson
Project Editor Amanda Wyatt
US Editor Megan Douglass
US Executive Editor Lori Cates Hand
Managing Editor Lisa Gillespie
Managing Art Editor Owen Peyton Jones
Production Editor Gillian Reid
Senior Production Controller Meskerem Berhane
Jacket Designer Akiko Kato
Jacket Design Development Manager Sophia MTT
Publisher Andrew Macintyre
Associate Publishing Director Liz Wheeler
Art Director Karen Self
Publishing Director Jonathan Metcalf

DK Delhi

Project Editor Neha Ruth Samuel
Senior Art Editor Vikas Chauhan
Project Picture Researcher Deepak Negi
Managing Editor Kingshuk Ghoshal
Managing Art Editor Govind Mittal
Senior DTP Designer Neeraj Bhatia
DTP Designer Jaypal Chauhan
Pre-Production Manager Balwant Singh
Production Manager Pankaj Sharma
Jacket Designers Suhita Dharamjit, Pooja Pipil

First Edition

Project Editor Matt Turner
Project Art Editor Keith Davis
Senior Editor Fran Jones
Senior Art Editor Stefan Podhorodecki
Category Publisher Linda Martin
Managing Art Editor Jane Thomas
Picture Researcher Marie Osborn
DK Picture Library Jonathan Brookes
Production Jenny Jacoby
DTP Designer Siu Yin Ho

This American Edition, 2020
First American Edition, 2003
Published in the United States by DK Publishing
1450 Broadway, Suite 801, New York, NY 10018

The catalog record for this book is available from the Library of Congress.
ISBN 978-1-4654-9757-4 (Paperback)
ISBN 978-1-4654-9847-2 (Hardcover)

DK books are available at special discounts when purchased in bulk
for sales promotions, premiums, fund-raising, or educational use.
For details, contact: DK Publishing Special Markets,
1450 Broadway, Suite 801, New York, NY 10018
SpecialSales@dk.com

Printed and bound in the UK

For the curious
www.dk.com

MIX
Paper from
responsible sources
FSC™ C018179

Note to Parents
Every effort has been made to ensure that the information in this book is as up-to-date as possible at the time of
going to press. The internet, by its very nature, is liable to change. Homepage and website content is constantly
being updated, as well as website addresses. In addition, websites may contain material or links to material that may
be unsuitable for children. The publishers, therefore, cannot accept responsibility for any third party websites or any
material contained in or linked to the same or for any consequences arising from use of the internet; nor can the
publishers guarantee that any website or URLs featured in this book will be as shown. Parents are strongly advised
to ensure that access to the internet by children is supervised by a responsible adult.

CONTENTS

INTRODUCTION

Over a century ago, on windswept sand dunes on the Atlantic coast of the United States, Orville Wright climbed into a homemade flying machine built of wood, cloth, piano wire, and bicycle chains. Lying flat on his stomach, Orville lifted from the ground and flew for 12 seconds before coming down with a bump. And that was the beginning of aircraft flight!

Today, large numbers of people fly every year in airplanes that can stay airborne for hours and travel at speeds unimagined in Orville Wright's day. Astronauts venture into space and have journeyed as far as the moon. So how did people turn the dream of flying like birds into a reality? And once airborne, how did the pioneers of flight develop the incredible aircraft that we see today?

IS IT A PLANE OR A HELICOPTER? IT'S BOTH—AN AUTOGIRO OF THE EARLY 1900S.

FAST AND HIGHLY MANEUVERABLE, THE F-35 STEALTH COMBAT AIRCRAFT HAS SERVED THE UNITED STATES AIR FORCE SINCE 2016.

In the search for answers to these questions, you'll follow a story of heroic adventures—of people who crossed oceans and mountain ranges in tiny airplanes, or who pushed aircraft to the limits in the search for maximum speed. You'll learn what it was like to cruise in style in one of the great airships that once sailed the skies, or to pilot a rocket plane dropped like a bomb from another aircraft.

You'll also encounter some of the world's most extreme machines, from aircraft powered by bicycle pedals or sunlight to the mighty Saturn rocket that propelled astronauts on their course to the moon.

So, fasten your seat-belts for a thrilling trip through the story of flight!

TO FLY LIKE A BIRD

Have you ever secretly wished you could simply spread your arms and flap high into the sky, just like a bird? Dreams such as this led our ancestors to invent machines that really could take to the air. From their first daring attempts in balloons and gliders, the passion for powered flight fast took shape.

GREEK INVENTOR DAEDALUS FLIES ON HIS FEATHERED WINGS. MADE IN 1493, THIS IS THE FIRST PRINTED IMAGE OF HUMAN FLIGHT.

Birdlike wings
If you had lived in Berlin, Germany, in the late 1800s, you might have enjoyed a local attraction—the flights of the "birdman" Otto Lilienthal.

of 33–66 ft (10–20 m), before landing clumsily a few seconds later at the foot of the hill. Lilienthal was trying to fulfill an age-old human dream of flying like birds. If they could do it, then why couldn't we?

"BIRDMAN" LILIENTHAL MADE OVER 1,000 GLIDING FLIGHTS.

Before an awestruck crowd, the bearded Lilienthal stood on a hill with birdlike wings fitted to his body. Then he marched downhill into the wind with his wings spread until a gust lifted him into the air. He would soar over the spectators at a height

Coming unstuck
The ancient Greek myth of Daedalus and Icarus tells the story of a father and son who tried to escape imprisonment on the island of Crete. They used wings made of feathers stuck together with wax.

Daedalus succeeds in flying to freedom, but his son Icarus flies too close to the sun. The wax gluing his wings together melts, and Icarus plunges to his death.

Despite this discouraging tale, history is full of examples of people who have tried to fly. Most fixed crude wings to their arms and jumped off a tower or a cliff. All, like Icarus, came unstuck. Those that didn't die were badly injured.

Da Vinci's dreams

Even the great Italian inventor Leonardo da Vinci imagined that a person would be able to fly by flapping wings. Da Vinci lived about 500 years ago. The flying machines he sketched in his notebooks were based on his observation of birds and bats. He also drew a kind of helicopter. But Leonardo's machines were hopeless.

The trouble is that human bodies just aren't up to flapping flight. Birds have very light bodies, and the muscles that operate their wings are incredibly powerful in relation to their size. Lilienthal showed the best that could be achieved by attaching wings to arms— a short downhill glide.

OTTO LILIENTHAL TAKES OFF IN ONE OF HIS EARLY FLYING EXPERIMENTS. HE WAS SURE HUMANS COULD LEARN TO FLY BY COPYING BIRDS.

A load of hot air

The first people to succeed in becoming airborne, over 200 years ago, did so in a completely unbirdlike manner. They were a couple of brothers, Joseph and Etienne Montgolfier, paper manufacturers from the French town of Annonay. The Montgolfiers

A DUCK WAS ONE OF THE WORLD'S FIRST THREE BALLOONISTS, SENT UP BY THE MONTGOLFIER BROTHERS ON A TEST FLIGHT WITH A CHICKEN AND A SHEEP.

on a test flight before attempting a human ascent. On November 21, 1783, two brave Frenchmen, Pilâtre de Rozier and the Marquis d'Arlande, became the

IN 1812, BALLOONIST SOPHIE BLANCHARD FLEW OVER THE ALPS.

noticed that if you filled a paper bag with hot air by holding it over a fire, it would soar upward. This is because hot air is lighter than cold air. The bag of hot air rises in the same way that a cork bobs back to the surface if you place it under water.

The Montgolfiers reasoned that a big enough hot-air bag, or balloon, would lift something strapped underneath it—for example, a basket with people in it.

Farmyard fliers

The brothers built a series of large balloons. They sent up a duck, a chicken, and a sheep

first people to try a Montgolfier balloon. They climbed into the basket underneath it and rose from the ground. Feeding a fire in a straw-filled brazier to keep the bag filled with hot air, they stayed aloft for 25 minutes and traveled 5 miles (8 km) before returning safely to earth.

Popular pastime

Balloons really caught on. Hot air was soon mostly replaced by lighter-than-air gases such as hydrogen. Some balloonists made epic flights—for example, across the Channel from England to France in 1785. But the drawbacks of balloons were obvious. They were at the mercy of the weather, traveling wherever the wind blew them. And they needed a huge gas bag to carry just two or three people. Balloons were fun, but they weren't of much use.

Aim high!

As the 18th century drew to a close, however, one person started thinking a little further. Sir George Cayley was an English country gentleman from Yorkshire.

Cayley got his ideas from flying kites. He reasoned that if a balloon could carry people aloft, perhaps a kite could do the same. He tied a big kite across a pole, making the first aircraft wing. He added a movable tail to the end of the pole to create an "aircraft" which was able to go up and down and turn from side to side. From 1809, Cayley

AN "AERIAL STEAM CARRIAGE" FLIES OVER A CITY— A FANTASY IMAGE ADVERTISING A PROPOSED "STEAM AIRLINE" IN 1843.

began testing the aircraft, which on occasion carried a small boy for a few yards.

How planes fly

Cayley also published his thoughts on heavier-than-air flight. He explained the basic principles of lift, thrust, and drag. Lift is the upward force provided by the wing. It has to be sufficient to raise the weight of the aircraft and pilot. Thrust, the power driving the plane forward, has to be strong enough to overcome drag—the resistance of air to anything trying to advance through it.

Nobody really listened to Cayley's ideas. In any case, no one could think of a way to power an aircraft. Cayley's

WEIRD WORLD

IN 1853, SIR GEORGE CAYLEY MADE HIS COACHMAN FLY A SHORT DISTANCE IN A GLIDER. THE COACHMAN INSTANTLY QUIT HIS JOB, TELLING CAYLEY: "I WAS HIRED TO DRIVE, AND NOT TO FLY."

first idea was to propel his machine forward using oars, like a rowing boat!

Winging it

Without an engine, fliers could do no more than glide. Through the 1800s, countless experiments by people such as French sea captain Jean-Marie Le Bris and American engineer Octave Chanute showed how wings could be designed to increase lift. But Chanute's gliders could fly at most only a few hundred yards downhill.

More hot air

During the 1800s, steam engines came into use to power railroad locomotives and ships. Inventors thought of using steam to drive flying machines by turning a propeller. But steam engines were simply too heavy for flight. The most successful steam-powered flying machine was the *Éole*, a bat-winged design by French engineer Clément Ader. It managed just a few seconds in the air. Practical, powered, heavier-than-air flight needed a new kind of engine.

Invented in the 1880s, gasoline engines were much lighter than steam engines. They at last gave inventors a real chance of designing a flying machine that actually worked.

The Wright idea

In 1899, two brothers living in Ohio decided to try heavier-than-air flight. They were Wilbur and Orville Wright, and they ran a bicycle shop, making and selling their own bikes.

Having read everything that had been written about flying, the Wrights built a glider in their workshop. In the summer of 1900, they took

THIS IS ONE OF SIR GEORGE CAYLEY'S DESIGNS FOR A CREWED GLIDER. CAYLEY KNEW IN THEORY HOW TO FLY, BUT DOING IT IN PRACTICE WAS NOT SO EASY.

it to Kitty Hawk, a tiny settlement on the coast of North Carolina, and set up their camp in the windswept sand dunes.

of their experiments. Two more summers passed at Kitty Hawk, and by 1903 the brothers were ready to fit a gasoline engine to their glider.

WATCHED BY HIS BROTHER WILBUR, ORVILLE WRIGHT TAKES OFF ON THE FIRST FLIGHT AT KITTY HAWK ON DECEMBER 17, 1903.

WEIRD WORLD
THIS FAMOUS PHOTO OF THE WRIGHT BROTHERS' FIRST FLIGHT WAS SHOT BY KITTY HAWK RESIDENT JOHN DANIELS, WHO HAD NEVER TAKEN A PHOTOGRAPH BEFORE.

Learning the ropes

The Wright brothers' approach to flying was much more practical and methodical than anyone else's. Day after day they experimented with glider flights down the dunes, working out what went wrong each time they crashed. Gradually they learned to pilot the glider. They worked out how to control it in pitch (nose up or down), in yaw (from side to side), and in roll (wings going down on one side and up on the other).

For the winter they returned to their workshop and improved their glider based on the results

History is made

In September 1903 the Wrights took their *Flyer* to Kitty Hawk. They ran into many difficulties, though, and were almost beaten in the race to be first to fly. While the Wrights had been at work, Samuel Pierpont Langley, a famous American scientist, had spent a fortune in taxpayers' money on an official project to achieve the first manned heavier-than-air flight. Langley's large gasoline-driven flying machine, the *Aerodrome*, was ready by October 1903. But launched from the top of a houseboat on the Potomac River, it plunged straight into

This is perhaps understandable. After all, flying for less than a minute in sand dunes didn't sound great. But the Wrights knew that they had cracked it.

the water. A second attempt on December 8 failed in the same way, almost drowning the unfortunate pilot.

These failed attempts left the way open for the Wrights, and on December 17, 1903, they made four powered flights. The first, by Orville, lasted 12 seconds. The last, by Wilbur, covered 852 ft (260 m) in 59 seconds.

These first few powered flights are now the stuff of aviation legend, but at the time the newspapers made little fuss.

Over the next two years they improved their *Flyer* until they could make flights of over half an hour. It was not until 1908, when Wilbur demonstrated their aircraft to huge crowds in France, that the Wright brothers were finally credited with being the first to achieve sustained, controlled, heavier-than-air flight.

AMERICAN EDITH BERG PREPARES TO FLY ALONGSIDE WILBUR WRIGHT. PASSENGERS SIMPLY SAT ON THE WING AND HELD TIGHT.

UP, UP, AND AWAY

Would you have dared to fly in a rickety little plane powered by a motorcycle engine? The early aviators must have had boundless courage, for the first true flying machines had a nasty habit of killing their pilots. Nevertheless, the pioneering spirit made sure there was a constant stream of pilots prepared to risk all for the glory.

LOUIS BLERIOT'S FLYING HELMET WAS A CRUDE EAR-WARMER, BUT VITAL IN AN OPEN COCKPIT.

On a wing and a prayer
On the morning of July 25, 1909, a man with a droopy mustache and a tight-fitting cap climbed into the seat of an aircraft in a field on the north coast of France. The aviator Louis Blériot

A THREE-CYLINDER MOTORCYCLE ENGINE POWERED THE TYPE XI PLANE FLOWN BY BLERIOT IN JULY 1909.

BLERIOT'S WORRIED WIFE LATER BANNED HIM FROM FLYING.

was setting out to win a £1,000 ($4,870) prize put up by a British newspaper for the first person to fly over the Channel to England. Although the distance was only 20 miles (32 km), it was a desperate venture in a flimsy aircraft made of wood, wire, and fabric, and powered by a crude motorcycle engine.

Close call

Blériot took off and vanished into the morning mist, flying low over the sea at about 30 mph (48 km/h). He had no compass and almost missed England completely. Luckily, after about 20 minutes he spotted the white cliffs of Dover. He landed in a field near Dover Castle, with a crunch that smashed the wheels on his plane.

Journey to glory

Blériot's flight, though just over 36 minutes long, caused a stir. Few people had believed that an aircraft could ever fly across water from country to country. Blériot was a hero and Europe went flight crazy.

Until the Channel crossing, flight was only of real interest to a handful of enthusiasts—people like Blériot himself and the Wright brothers. A month after Blériot's flight, when almost all the pilots in the world showed up for the first ever air show at Reims, in eastern France, there were just 22 of them.

Yet over half a million people came to see the fliers in action. There were plenty of thrills and spills—one pilot flew into a haystack—but most people were just amazed to see aircraft fly at all.

Flying fever

Over the next few years, hundreds of adventurous young people learned to fly. They were

Air races

Long-distance races were staged—from London to Manchester,

drawn by the excitement of flight and by the chance of fame. Huge crowds attended air shows, and excitement rose to fever pitch during record-breaking, long-distance flights by the daring aviators. These included Georges Chavez, who became the first person to fly over the Alps in 1910, and Roland Garros, who flew across the Mediterranean Sea from France to North Africa in 1913.

THOMAS SELFRIDGE WAS THE FIRST PERSON TO DIE IN AN AIR CRASH, KILLED WHEN FLYING IN A PLANE PILOTED BY ORVILLE WRIGHT ON SEPTEMBER 17, 1908.

from Paris to Madrid, from Paris to Rome. These were pretty chaotic events. To avoid getting lost, pilots mostly

from coast to coast. It took him seven weeks and 18 crashes to get from New York to California! His wife followed him by train and nursed him back to health after each crash.

FRENCH PILOT LOUIS PAULHAN, FLYING A FARMAN BIPLANE, ON HIS WAY TO WINNING THE 1910 LONDON–MANCHESTER AIR RACE. THERE WERE ONLY TWO CONTESTANTS FOR THE HEFTY PRIZE OF £10,000 ($48,600).

followed roads or railroads. If they did lose their way, which happened frequently, they landed in a field and asked for directions. Often no more than two or three fliers completed the race, and the countryside was strewn with the mangled wreckage of aircraft that didn't make the distance.

In 1911, the American Cal Rodgers took up a challenge to fly across the United States

FIRST AVIATION MEETING IN ENGLAND.

CODY
DELAGRANGE
FARMAN
SOMMER
LEBLON
MOLON
PREVOT
DE LA VAUX
& OTHER
AVIATORS ENGAGED.

DONCASTER
15TH TO 23RD OCTOBER 1909.

COLORFUL POSTERS ADVERTISED THE AIR SHOWS WHERE MOST PEOPLE CAUGHT THEIR FIRST EXCITING GLIMPSE OF AN AIRPLANE.

Safety last
Flying was incredibly dangerous in these pioneering days. Pilots rarely wore seat-belts. Passengers either sat on the wing and held onto one of the struts, or squeezed in behind the pilot, as if they were on the back of a motorcycle. All too often the engines

broke down. Luckily, early aircraft could glide well without power, giving the pilot time to look for a clear space to land. But early aircraft were also flimsy. Sometimes a wing simply fell off in flight, and that was usually fatal.

Flying was uncomfortable, too. Cockpits were open to the elements. Pilots froze in cold weather and got soaked when it rained. In many aircraft the engines sprayed the pilots with stinking castor oil.

Sticks and string

All early aircraft were made of wood, cloth, and piano wire, and were built by hand in small workshops. They also all had gasoline engines and propellers. But in other ways their designs varied wildly as inventors experimented with different approaches. Some flying machines had the propeller at the back, others at the front. Some, known as monoplanes, had one wing while others had two (biplanes) or even three (triplanes). Some back-to-front, so-called "canard" designs, had the "tail" in front of the pilot. Many looked as though they shouldn't fly at all— and some of them didn't.

Two are better than one

Gradually, biplanes with a propeller at the front became the norm. Monoplanes were faster because they had fewer of the struts and wires that created so much drag. But the two wings of a biplane

THE BALCONY ON THE NOSE OF THE *ILYA MUROMETS* MULTI-ENGINED AIRCRAFT GAVE A GREAT, IF WINDY, VIEW.

gave double the lift. Even more importantly, biplanes could be made safer. Monoplanes tended to fall apart if the pilot turned too tightly!

Faster, higher ...

The progress made in the first 10 years of the age of flight could be measured in speed. In 1903, the Wright *Flyer* had traveled at 30 mph (48 km/h), but by 1914 the world speed record was 92 mph (147 km/h).

FRENCH AVIATION PIONEER HÉLÈNE DUTRIEU SITS IN THE OPEN-AIR PILOT SEAT OF HER BIPLANE.

WEIRD WORLD
THE FIRST PARACHUTE JUMP FROM AN AIRPLANE WAS MADE IN 1912. BUT THE BRITISH ARMY REFUSED TO GIVE ITS PILOTS PARACHUTES, CLAIMING THAT IT WOULD ENCOURAGE COWARDICE.

By then, pilots had flown up to 20,000 ft (6,100 m) above the ground. They had also learned to perform breathtaking stunts such as looping-the-loop. And there were now aircraft fitted with floats that took off and landed on lakes or oceans.

And larger
Designers were also building larger planes. In 1913, a young Russian engineer, Igor Sikorsky, designed the first aircraft with more than one engine. His *Ilya Muromets*, which flew the following year, had four engines and could carry 16 people. It was the first aircraft with a lavatory and electric lights. It also had an open balcony in the nose where you could stand to get a magnificent view.

From fun to fighting
Despite these advances, aircraft remained mostly fun. They were expensive, grown-up toys for sport and recreation. This all changed in 1914, when World War I broke out in Europe. During the four years that the fighting lasted, tens of thousands of aircraft were built to fight the war in the air. Many people would look back nostalgically to the innocent times before flying machines became killing machines.

21

THE GOLDEN AGE

The 1920s and 1930s are often called the "golden age of flight." This was a time when fliers were worshipped as cool, glamorous, death-defying heroes, and could become as famous as monarchs or movie stars. Keeping them in the air were the latest aircraft designs, which flew ever farther, higher, and faster, and gradually made flying a safer, more comfortable way to travel.

CHARLES LINDBERGH INSPECTS THE ENGINE ON WHICH HIS LIFE DEPENDED BEFORE HIS ATLANTIC FLIGHT.

Daring adventure
The most famous flier of the "golden age" was Charles Lindbergh, but on May 20, 1927, he was still just another unknown American pilot. That day he set off from New York in the hope of becoming the first person to fly nonstop to Paris.

Lindbergh nearly crashed on takeoff because his aircraft was so heavy, full to the brim with gasoline for the long flight. Once in the air he was totally alone. He had no radio. All he had in his cramped cockpit was a clock, an unreliable compass, a water bottle, and five sandwiches. His ears were stuffed with cotton to keep out the deafening noise of the engine, and his view to the front was blocked by a large fuel tank. But he had a quiet determination to succeed.

22

Slim chance

People thought Lindbergh was crazy to try the 3,600-mile (5,796-km) flight solo and in a plane with only one engine. Just the

LINDBERGH'S AIRCRAFT WAS NAMED AFTER HIS SPONSORS—A GROUP OF BUSINESSMEN IN ST. LOUIS, MISSOURI.

The most dangerous part of the flight was crossing the Atlantic Ocean. For 15 hours Lindbergh was out of sight of land, with no hope of rescue if his engine failed and forced him to land in the hostile ocean.

Through the night Lindbergh fought desperately to stay awake—if he fell asleep his aircraft would

LINDBERGH YELLED DOWN TO A SHIP: "WHICH WAY IS IRELAND?"

week before, two skilled French fliers, Francois Coli and Charles Nungesser, had disappeared on the way from Paris to New York. What chance did Lindbergh have?

IN MAY 1932, FAMOUS AMERICAN FLIER AMELIA EARHART BECAME THE FIRST WOMAN TO FLY SOLO ACROSS THE ATLANTIC.

dive out of control. At moments he flew down dangerously close to the waves so that the icy spray on his face would keep him alert.

Lucky Lindy

Amazingly, Lindbergh not only stayed awake, but found his way across the featureless ocean. And his engine didn't let him down. When he landed in Paris, almost 34 hours after taking off, he was greeted with one of the wildest reception parties ever seen. The French called him "Lucky Lindy," though skill and sheer courage had been just as important.

Death or glory

Although no one could quite match Lindbergh's fame, plenty of other adventurers were prepared to risk their lives for fame and fortune. Every country had its heroes. The British celebrated John Alcock and Arthur Brown, who made the first

nonstop flight across the Atlantic in 1919—they landed nose down in an Irish bog. There were female flying stars, too; none more famous than America's Amelia Earhart, who became the first woman to fly solo across the

A STUNT FLIER BALANCES ABOVE A COCKPIT IN MID-AIR. STUNTS LIKE THIS WERE EXTREMELY DANGEROUS.

Atlantic in 1932. Perhaps the strangest of the celebrities was Douglas Corrigan, who set out to fly from New York to California in 1938, but got lost soon after take off and instead landed in Ireland. "Wrong Way Corrigan" was the toast of America!

Barnstorming

What made flying so exciting was the risk. In the United States, many pilots

ONE OF THE MOST DARING
BARNSTORMERS WAS POPULAR AFRICAN
AMERICAN PILOT BESSIE COLEMAN.

made a living as touring "barnstormers." They would put on incredible flying shows full of crazy stunts. A pilot might climb out of the cockpit while flying high above the ground and do handstands on the wing, or climb from one aircraft to another and back again in flight. To excite the crowds, barnstormers staged crashes, deliberately flying into buildings, or pretended to fall out of their aircraft by accident, not pulling their parachute ripcord until the very last moment. Some barnstormers gained national fame, like African American Bessie Coleman, who was affectionately known as "Queen Bess." They accepted danger in a devil-may-care spirit—one flier quipped that they were so badly paid, the worst risk was dying of starvation!

WEIRD WORLD

ONE 1920s BARNSTORMING GROUP LISTED FEES FOR STUNTS: $250 TO STAGE A BOXING BOUT ON A WING; $1,200 TO HIT A HOUSE; $1,500 TO BLOW UP A PLANE IN MID-AIR.

Racing demons

The US National Air Races excited massive interest as weird and wonderful things happened at the events. Pilot Roscoe Turner flew with a pet lion cub in his cockpit—it had its own parachute!

There were some outlandish aircraft, too, designed for speed and nothing else. The Gee Bee Racer, for instance, was just a huge engine with stubby wings attached. It was incredibly hard to fly—five pilots were killed trying to master it. But ace pilot Jimmy Doolittle flew one to victory at the National Air Races in 1932 at an average speed of 296 mph (476 km/h).

a limitless runway. At the annual Schneider Trophy seaplane race in 1931, a Supermarine became the first aircraft to fly at over 400 mph (644 km/h)— faster than any human had ever traveled before.

IN 1932, AN ENGLAND-AUSTRALIA FLIGHT TOOK OVER EIGHT DAYS.

Landing on sea

At the time, though, the fastest aircraft in the world were seaplanes. Few airstrips had yet been built on land, and in any case the water provided

Flying all over the world

But flight was not just for kicks. Fliers trailblazed routes that would one day be used for regular passenger flights. They flew over deserts and great mountain ranges, down the length of Africa, and across Central Asia, bringing contact with the outside world to

SUPERMARINE PUBLICIZES THE SUCCESS OF ITS RACING SEAPLANES. REGINALD MITCHELL, WHO DESIGNED PLANES FOR THE COMPANY, LATER CREATED THE SPITFIRE FIGHTER.

THE GEE BEE WAS ONE OF THE FASTEST PLANES OF THE 1930S. HERE, A PILOT FLIES A RESTORED GEE BEE UPSIDE DOWN OVER THE SOUTHWESTERN UNITED STATES.

was a great relief when the first "flying doctor" service started. At last, you could call for urgent medical care that might arrive in time to save a life. In many parts of the globe, air mail brought regular delivery of letters for the first time—another lifeline to the outside world.

places without roads, railroads, or telephones.

The fliers were not always welcome. When famous French pilot Jean Mermoz was forced to crash-land in the Sahara Desert, he was captured by tribesmen, who only let him go after a ransom was paid.

Air rescue

Aircraft had important uses in remote places. If you lived on a remote farm in the Australian outback during the 1920s, it

Pioneers in peril

Every pilot who took part in extending flight across the world had their close shaves. Many lost their lives, especially flying over the empty oceans. Australia's most famous flier, Charles Kingsford Smith, disappeared in the Indian Ocean while flying

IN THE 1930S, HUGE WIND-TUNNELS WERE BUILT TO TEST NEW AIRCRAFT DESIGNS.

leap forward in the way aircraft were designed. Clumsy contraptions of canvas, wood, and wire were on the way out. In their place were sleek new machines of smooth, shiny aluminum and steel.

from England to Australia in 1935. Jean Mermoz disappeared over the South Atlantic Ocean in 1936. Amelia Earhart vanished in the Pacific while attempting a round-the-world flight in 1937. Hundreds of fliers suffered similar fates, but they proved that long-distance flight was a reality.

Designers and engineers

The pilots could not have done what they did without the efforts of aircraft designers and engineers, who made airplanes that flew faster and farther than ever before.

The design of aircraft engines kept getting more powerful and much more reliable. A 1930s aircraft engine might generate 10 or 20 times more power than in the early days of the 20th century. There was also a great

What a drag

It was German plane-maker Hugo Junkers who worked out how to make monoplanes with metal wings that did not need struts or wires to hold them firm. These new streamlined monoplanes slipped through the air with less drag (resistance).

In the wind

Using giant wind-tunnels, engineers found other ways to reduce drag. They proved, for instance, that having the wheels sticking out all the time in flight added unwanted drag. So aircraft were built with retractable undercarriages—the wheels pulled up into the fuselage (main body of aircraft)

28

or wings after take off and were lowered again for landing. This made an enormous improvement to the performance of aircraft.

Flying on auto

With better aircraft came better instruments to help pilots fly them. Until the 1930s, most pilots flew "by the seat of their pants," trusting their instincts more than the dials in their cockpit which were as likely to be wrong as right.

But even experienced pilots admitted that flying at night or in heavy cloud was safer when you had radio, a compass that really worked, and an "artificial horizon" dial to show you which way up you were. When one-eyed American pilot Wiley Post

flew solo around the world in 1933 he had a device known as an automatic pilot in his aircraft, which held the plane steady and level while he took a nap.

End of an era

By the end of the 1930s, the golden age of air heroes was drawing to an end, because better aircraft and instruments were beginning to make flying reasonably safe. That's why, today, no one needs the courage and blind luck of Lindbergh to cross the Atlantic—just a passport and a ticket.

THE GERMAN FIRM JUNKERS WAS THE FIRST TO MAKE ALL-METAL AIRCRAFT, LIKE THIS THREE-ENGINED 1930S AIRLINER.

SHIPS OF THE AIR

About four times the size of a jumbo jet, the Hindenburg was the largest aircraft ever to fly. It was the most celebrated of the airships, which offered rich passengers a luxurious cruise in an era when planes were widely seen as dangerous toys. If airships had not turned out to be even more unsafe, the future of air travel might well have been cigar-shaped.

Lap of luxury

The *Hindenburg* was more like a ship than a plane. It was steered by a man standing at a nautical wheel, while dozens of crew hurried along gangways inside its silver-gray skin.

In the 1930s, the *Hindenburg* carried passengers from Europe to North America. The trip took two to three days, but what it lacked in speed, it made up for in style. Next time you sit in an

SERVERS PREPARE TO SERVE TEA IN THE LUXURIOUS DINING ROOM OF THE BRITISH AIRSHIP *R100*.

airline seat, eating a meal off a tray, picture yourself as a passenger on the *Hindenburg*.

You could stroll on the promenade deck and peer down through sloping windows to the ocean. The distant engine hum was broken only by the sounding of a gong calling you to dinner. You would use the finest white linen and silver cutlery, while waiters served you a gourmet meal and a pianist tinkled away at a piano. When you felt tired, you could retire to bed in your own cozy cabin, or freshen up under a hot shower.

flammable. All it needed was a stray spark and a slight gas leak—and then *whoomph!*

The gasbags of the *Hindenburg* were made from a material known as goldbeater's skin, used because it did not create sparks. Goldbeater's skin may sound fancy, but it's actually just

WEIRD WORLD
THE AIRSHIP *HINDENBURG* HAD ITS OWN DAILY NEWSPAPER PRINTED ON BOARD SO PASSENGERS COULD READ THE LATEST NEWS AT BREAKFAST.

Deadly gasbags
But there was a downside to all this. Most of the *Hindenburg's* bulk consisted of huge bags filled with hydrogen, a lighter-than-air gas that kept the airship aloft. Hydrogen is highly

THE GERMAN AIRSHIP *HINDENBURG* BORE THE SWASTIKA, THE SYMBOL OF THE NAZI REGIME THAT THEN RULED GERMANY.

the lining of a cow's stomach. It took a million stomach linings to make the gasbags for a single airship!

31

AN AIRSHIP BEING BUILT SHOWS THE LIGHTWEIGHT ALUMINUM-ALLOY FRAME USUALLY HIDDEN BY ITS OUTER ENVELOPE.

Not even a million cows could make hydrogen safe to use. Helium would have been a much safer gas; it was lighter than air, and it didn't burn. But the only source of helium in the world was in Texas, and the United States wouldn't share it. Everyone else had to make do with hydrogen gas.

Early risers

Despite the safety problem, airships had long held the lead over airplanes. The first powered flight was made not by the Wrights, but by French engineer Henri Giffard.

Tower—and this was at a time when the Wright brothers were still testing gliders.

Zeppelin

The man whose name is forever associated with airships was Count Zeppelin, a German aristocrat. He built his first airship in 1900, and by 1910 had developed his "zeppelins" until they were reliable enough to carry sightseers on trips.

In World War I, zeppelins found a more sinister use. Chugging through the night skies across the North Sea, German airships dropped bombs on London and other parts of England. They caused a great deal of fear but not much damage, and many were shot down in flames.

In 1852, he fitted a small steam engine to a balloon and steered his "dirigible" around the sky.

In 1901, Brazilian-born Parisian Alberto Santos-Dumont flew an airship for half an hour around the Eiffel

HENRI GIFFARD'S STEAM-POWERED DIRIGIBLE FLEW AT ABOUT 5 MPH (8 KM/H) IN STILL AIR—IT COULDN'T MAKE ANY HEADWAY INTO THE WIND.

Aircraft carriers

After World War I, the United States Navy became interested in airships, which they wanted

33

to use as airborne aircraft carriers. This idea was not quite as silly as it might sound now.

The Navy planned to hook half a dozen small fighter aircraft onto the underside of an airship. When it was time for a mission, a pilot would climb into one of the fighters and the hook was released to launch it. When the fighter returned it would hook onto the airship again in flight—this was a tricky maneuver, but not impossible.

Unfit for duty

The reason the "airborne aircraft carrier" idea didn't work was because the US Navy couldn't make its airships safe, even with helium instead of hydrogen. In a howling gale or a storm, airships were bad places to be. They just kept crashing. Eventually, the US Navy gave up on them.

Britain, too, had a catastrophic experience with airships. In October 1930, a new British airship, R101, set off on its maiden flight from England to India with a lot of VIPs on board for the special occasion. It got no further than France. On a night of wind and rain it crashed into a hillside, killing 48 of the 54 people on board.

German airships

In Germany, airships had more success. In 1929, the *Graf Zeppelin* carried 53 passengers and crew on a three-week journey right around the world. Along with the even bigger *Hindenburg*, the *Graf Zeppelin* allowed for regular and reliable—though immensely expensive—services across the Atlantic.

The Germans believed that the future of air travel was gas-filled, and some Americans agreed with them. New York's Empire State Building was built with a docking mast for airships at its tip. But their optimism was soon to be crushed.

A 150-FT (46-M) MOORING MAST FOR AIRSHIPS ONCE FORMED THE TOP OF NEW YORK'S EMPIRE STATE BUILDING.

Disaster!

The zeppelin's future ended suddenly on the evening of May 6, 1937. The *Hindenburg* had arrived at Lakehurst, New Jersey, after a regular run from Europe. As it docked, a lick of flame appeared at the stern. The probable cause was a spark of static electricity

THE *HINDENBURG* BURNS IN 1937. SPARKS OF STATIC ELECTRICITY ON THE FLAMMABLE SKIN MAY HAVE STARTED THE FIRE.

igniting the paint on the skin. The gas then caught fire, resulting in an inferno. Amazingly, 62 of the 97 people on board survived. Even more might have lived had they waited for the airship to sink a little. Instead, many leaped off at once in panic.

The *Hindenburg* disaster was the end of airship travel. Linked in people's imaginations with the idea of a fiery death, airships became mostly extinct, like dinosaurs of the skies.

WEIRD WORLD

OUT OF THE FIRST 161 AIRSHIPS BUILT, 60 WERE DESTROYED IN ACCIDENTS. IF MODERN AIRLINERS WERE THAT ACCIDENT-PRONE, IT'S ESTIMATED THAT THERE WOULD BE 12 AIR CRASHES A DAY!

35

TRAVELING IN STYLE

In the early days of air travel, flying was a genuine adventure for the few passengers who tried it. They needed strong nerves and a strong stomach, as well as a healthy bank balance. But if there was discomfort, there was style and luxury as well, until progress in aircraft design and air traffic control made air travel what it is today— safe, easy, but also a little less fun.

PASSENGERS BOARD A FORD TRIMOTOR, THE "TIN GOOSE," THAT WAS AMERICA'S TOP AIRLINER IN THE 1920S.

Hot and bothered

It's the 1920s and you're crossing the United States in a Ford "Tin Goose," the very latest in airliner design.

A dozen passengers are sitting in two rows of wicker chairs. It's a hot day and they're sweating in the small passenger cabin—if it was winter they'd be shivering in overcoats.

Fortunately, they can open the windows for some fresh air— but this also lets in the full roar of the three engines. Even with the windows shut the engine noise is deafening, like sitting next to a pneumatic drill— which is why you're given earplugs when you board.

You must remember not to throw things out of the windows, especially over towns. People on the ground need to watch out, too, particularly since

PASSENGERS HAD TO BE WEIGHED AS WELL AS THEIR LUGGAGE, TO MAKE SURE THE PLANE WASN'T OVERLOADED.

PASSENGERS ON A SCENIC FLIGHT OVER LAKE GENEVA IN 1929 KEEP THEIR COATS ON IN THE DRAFTY AIRPLANE.

everything that goes into the lavatory falls straight out through a hole in the bottom of the fuselage!

Sick and shaken

The flight is much worse in bad weather. Then the plane bumps around like a carnival ride. Passengers are soon filling their "burp cups" with vomit—and this can go on for hours. (The first flight attendants employed in 1930 were qualified nurses to look after airsick passengers.)

If the weather gets too bad to fly, the pilot makes an emergency landing at a small airstrip or even on a farm field, and the shaken passengers finish their trip by train, probably relieved to be back on the ground.

Where are we?

Regular passenger services by airplane had started in Europe in 1919. But as you've seen, early air travel was not comfortable—and it wasn't that safe, either. In the

AIR TRAFFIC CONTROL 1920S STYLE: AN OFFICIAL WAVES A RED FLAG TO TELL AN AIRLINE PILOT THAT THE RUNWAY IS NOT YET CLEAR.

1920s, pilots still mostly followed roads or railroads to find their way, especially in low cloud or fog. Cutting across country was a recipe for getting utterly lost. And if two pilots were following the same road or railroad in opposite directions—ouch! The only form of air traffic control was at airfields,

Once airliners were fitted with radios they could talk to controllers at airports, who cleared them to take off or land. And so aircraft could travel safely by night, lines of giant beacons were set up along major airways, like lighthouses shining powerful beams high into the sky.

PASSENGERS SOMETIMES HAD TO LEAN OVER TO HELP PLANES TURN.

where a person waved a green flag to show it was safe to land and a red flag if it wasn't.

Lighting the way

Of course, things had to improve. By the 1930s, in Europe and the United States, proper airports were being built and "airways" were marked out—routes for airliners to follow from city to city.

Smoothing out the bumps

New aircraft made journeys quicker and more comfortable. The Douglas DC-3, launched in 1936, carried 21 passengers across the United States from coast to coast in about 18 hours, operating overnight and in most weather

Islander

PASSENGERS ON WEEK-LONG FLYING-BOAT JOURNEYS IN THE 1930S SOMETIMES SLEPT IN BUNKS AND WERE SERVED AN ELEGANT BREAKFAST IN BED.

conditions. Reasonable sound-proofing and shock absorbers made the seating less bone-shaking. There were in-flight meals much like we have today, but no entertainment. Though not appealing enough to tempt most people away from rail travel, it was a start.

By air and water

If you wanted to fly across oceans or to remote lands in the 1930s, you went by flying boat. These beautiful machines had wings attached to what was basically a boat hull. When they landed on water they hit with a thump, and spray splashed the windows. But people on ocean journeys felt safer in an aircraft that could land on the sea.

Flying boats opened up new routes, from England to South Africa for example, and from the United States to Hong Kong. These journeys could take from a few days to more than a week. In the evening

BECAUSE OF THEIR LARGE HULLS, FLYING BOATS LIKE THIS SHORT SUNDERLAND WERE MUCH MORE SPACIOUS INSIDE THAN AIRLINERS THAT OPERATED FROM LAND.

INTERNATIONAL AIR
TRAVEL GREW FOURFOLD
IN THE FIRST TEN YEARS
THAT THE BOEING 707
WAS IN SERVICE.

the flying boats might refuel on a Pacific island lagoon or on a lake in the heart of Africa, and the passengers would spend the night at a hotel. In Africa, they sometimes had to clear hippos out of the way before taking off the following morning. Traveling by flying boat was a special experience, enjoyed mostly by the wealthy few.

Pressure to succeed

In the 1940s, airliners headed for the heights. For the first time they had pressurized cabins, like today's large airliners. This could ride above clouds and storms, making flight much more comfortable.

By the 1950s airliners were large enough to carry 100 people and fly across oceans in a single hop. They landed at modern international airports, relying on proper air traffic control and radar (a system that sends out high-frequency radio waves to detect objects by listening for their echoes). But long-distance flying was still too costly.

meant that passengers could be carried high above Earth's surface, in the thin air of the stratosphere. Windows could no longer be opened, but aircraft

The age of jet travel

When jet-powered airliners arrived, long-distance travel really took off. The Boeing 707, which began flights across the Atlantic in 1958, traveled at up to 600 mph (960 km/h), twice as fast as propeller airliners. It halved the time it took to fly from New York to London or Paris—and reduced the journey's cost, too.

Mass transportation

Now that flying was easy and relatively inexpensive, it was within the reach of people who had never before dreamed of taking to the air. By the start of the 21st century, jet airliners worldwide were carrying more than a billion passengers a year. No one thought it odd to hop on a plane for a vacation in New York or New Zealand. No two cities on the planet were more than 24 hours apart.

Juan Trippe, the boss of PanAm, the first airline to use the Boeing 707, described the new era neatly: "We have shrunken the Earth."

THE FUTURISTIC LOOK OF LOS ANGELES AIRPORT SUMS UP THE DISTANCE AIR TRAVEL HAS COME SINCE THE ERA OF THE "TIN GOOSE" AND THE RED WARNING FLAG.

WEIRD WORLD

HARTSFIELD-JACKSON ATLANTA AIRPORT IN GEORGIA, THE WORLD'S BUSIEST AIRPORT, SERVED MORE THAN 100 MILLION PASSENGERS IN 2019, WHICH IS ABOUT 300,000 TRAVELERS A DAY.

WINGS FOR VICTORY

I t is sad but true that one of the major uses of aircraft has been for war. Early airplanes were so unreliable and difficult to fly that they were more likely to kill their pilots than anyone else. But over time warplanes became fearsomely powerful machines, armed with an array of bombs, missiles, and guns. The fighter pilots of two World Wars were popular heroes.

IN 1914, THE TECHNIQUE OF DROPPING BOMBS WAS PRIMITIVE. EVEN FLYING AT LOW LEVEL, YOU WERE UNLIKELY TO HIT A PRECISE TARGET.

Don't frighten the horses
When aircraft were first invented, wars were still fought by soldiers on horseback or on foot. Some old-fashioned army officers wanted nothing to do with the newfangled

that even the primitive aircraft of those days might be of use in warfare. Moving fast and flying high, they could act as "eyes in the sky," reporting back on enemy movements. And they might be able to drop things on the enemy— bombs, for example.

IN 1918 MORE AMERICAN PILOTS DIED TRAINING THAN FIGHTING.

flying machines—they were afraid that the noise of the engines might frighten their horses. But it was obvious

So, on the whole, those in the military welcomed the new invention, even if they weren't sure how helpful it would be.

42

The first warplanes

Between 1914 and 1918, the whole of Europe was engulfed in World War I. Millions of soldiers went off to battle, and so did a few hundred flimsy aircraft. While the soldiers dug

they dropped a bomb by hand over the side of the plane.

To guard its forces, each side sent up planes to shoot down the enemy. At first, pilots fired at one another with pistols or rifles, but it was not long before airplanes went up equipped with machine-guns.

A WORLD WAR I "DOGFIGHT" IS STAGED BETWEEN AN ALLIED S.E.5A BIPLANE AND THE FAMOUS RED FOKKER TRIPLANE (TOP) FLOWN BY GERMAN ACE BARON MANFRED VON RICHTHOFEN.

These planes were the first fighter aircraft.

into trenches, the aircraft flew overhead, taking photographs of their positions. Sometimes

Dogfights

Fighters spent most of their time shooting down almost defenseless reconnaissance or bomber aircraft. But sometimes they engaged in "dogfights," air battles in which dozens of fighter aircraft dodged and dived, trying to get an enemy in their sights without being shot down themselves.

Journalists hailed the fighter pilots as "knights of the air." The top pilots, called "aces," became legendary heroes.

The Red Baron

None was more famous than the German Baron Manfred von Richthofen. Known as the Red Baron, he was credited with 80 "kills." Richthofen's fighter squadron was nicknamed "Richthofen's Flying Circus," because all the aircraft were painted in different bright colors. But like many other aces, Richthofen was killed in action before the war was over.

The bombing menace

By the time World War I ended in 1918, it had involved tens of thousands of aircraft.

In a frightening development, airplanes and airships had started to bomb towns and cities. Only relatively small numbers of people were killed, because the aircraft were not powerful enough to carry many bombs over a long distance. But these air raids were terrifying for ordinary people. They knew that if there was ever another major war, aircraft

WEIRD WORLD

REGINALD MITCHELL, THE SPITFIRE'S DESIGNER, HATED THE PLANE'S "SILLY NAME." IT COULD HAVE BEEN WORSE—THE SAME FIRM CALLED ANOTHER PLANE THE SHREW!

AT THE TIME OF THE BATTLE OF BRITAIN, IN THE SUMMER OF 1940, THE SPITFIRE WAS THE ONLY BRITISH FIGHTER THAT COULD MATCH THE PERFORMANCE OF THE BEST GERMAN AIRCRAFT.

would play an even bigger role, and bombing of cities was likely to happen on a terrifying scale.

Terror from the skies

During the 1930s, Nazi Germany's Luftwaffe became the most feared air force in the world. Luftwaffe is a German word meaning "air weapon," and its deadly power was revealed when pilots and aircraft were sent to join in a civil war that raged in Spain.

In 1937, Luftwaffe dive-bombers attacked the small town of Guernica in Spain's Basque region. Many people were killed and half of the town was destroyed.

Air battle

When World War II broke out in 1939, bringing Britain and France into conflict with Nazi Germany, millions of British children were evacuated from cities to the countryside for fear of bombing. In the summer of 1940, the Battle of Britain was fought, the first battle to take place exclusively in the air.

THE MESSERSCHMITT BF 109 WAS THE SPITFIRE'S ARCH-ENEMY IN THE AIR DUELS OF THE BATTLE OF BRITAIN.

The Luftwaffe tried to destroy Britain's Royal Air Force (RAF) by bombing its airfields. German fighters escorted their slow bombers in order to protect them from RAF planes.

Luckily for the RAF, it had a new invention—radar—to detect incoming aircraft. Radar gave the RAF early warning of air raids, enabling it to "scramble" its fighters into the air to meet the intruders.

RAF Spitfires and Hurricanes took on Messerschmitt fighters and their fleets of bombers in the skies over southern England. Usually outnumbered, the RAF kept on fighting until the Luftwaffe had to accept it couldn't win control of the air. British prime minister Winston Churchill celebrated the RAF's

A LUFTWAFFE BOMBER CREW IN THEIR CRAMPED COCKPIT PREPARE TO RELEASE THEIR BOMBS OVER BRITAIN DURING A NIGHT RAID.

pilots in a famous phrase:
"Never had so much been
owed by so many to so few."

Cities under fire

The Germans then turned to
attacking British cities by night.
This was called the "Blitz."
Whenever the bombers
came over, a
warning
sounded and
people took
cover in air raid shelters.
Londoners slept on
Underground station
platforms to avoid the bombs.

The German raids caused
great damage and killed many
thousands of people. But
German cities eventually
suffered far more heavily.

Allies strike back

Like the Luftwaffe, the RAF
bombed by night. At first, lost
in the dark, its bombers could

rarely hit the right city, let
alone a particular district. Later
planes were fitted with radar
and radio to navigate at night.

German defenders also used
radar on their antiaircraft guns
and night fighters to find the
raiders, meaning battles were
fought between enemies who
saw one another only as blips
on a screen.

AMERICA'S
B-17 BOMBER
WAS CALLED THE
"FLYING FORTRESS"
BECAUSE IT WAS DEFENDED BY THE
FIREPOWER OF 13 MACHINE GUNS.

RAF night raids became
bigger and bigger, often with
up to a thousand four-engined
bombers dropping millions of
pounds of explosives on their
targets in a single operation.

America enters the fray

After the United States
entered the war in 1941, its
aircraft bombed Germany

FACTORIES MASS-PRODUCED AIRCRAFT ON
A HUGE SCALE IN WORLD WAR II. MORE
THAN 12,000 OF THESE B-17S WERE BUILT.

in daylight. Boeing B-17 Flying Fortresses and B-24 Liberators bristled with guns for protection against the Luftwaffe fighters.

Operating mostly from air bases in eastern England, the American planes had a crew of up to 10 men. On the B-17, one gunner sat in a ball turret, hanging under the aircraft's belly. The bombers flew at high altitude, their crew wearing oxygen masks and heated suits to stave off the cold. Attacking in their hundreds, they scored many more direct hits than the RAF. German air defenses were strong, and thousands of bombers were shot down, but Germany suffered enormous damage and loss of life.

Carriers

Meanwhile, the war at sea had also become an air war. Navies were traditionally proud of their battleships—big armored vessels with powerful guns.

THE FEARSOME JAWS ON THIS CURTISS FIGHTER WERE THE SYMBOL OF THE "FLYING TIGERS," A GROUP OF US PILOTS WHO FOUGHT THE JAPANESE IN BURMA (MYANMAR) AND CHINA.

The idea that an aircraft could sink one of these warships had once been thought ridiculous. This was proved wrong by American air commander Billy Mitchell in 1921. He staged a demonstration in which his

Martin biplane bombers sank a captured German battleship, the supposedly "unsinkable" *Ostfriesland*, in a mere 21 minutes. This encouraged navies to add aircraft carriers, which allowed planes to take off and land at sea, to their fleets. Battleships were still seen as the main war-winners at sea, though.

dive-bombers eventually destroyed the Japanese carriers, while US fighters shot down the Japanese planes.

Kamikaze!

In the last year of the war, the Japanese adopted a desperate new tactic: suicide attacks. So-called kamikaze pilots flew their

Pearl Harbor

On December 7, 1941, the Japanese Navy Air service launched a surprise attack on the American naval base at Pearl Harbor in Hawaii. Japanese bombers and torpedo aircraft, launched from aircraft carriers, sank a large part of the US Pacific Fleet in a few hours, including five battleships. More than 2,400 personnel died.

Mitsubishi "Zero" and Aichi "Val" aircraft straight at US warships, aiming at points where their exploding bombs and fuel would cause the most damage, such as the aircraft hangars of carriers. They were also taught words to shout at the last moment in order to

EACH B-1 BOMBER COST ABOUT $200 MILLION TO BUILD.

The Pacific War between the United States and Japan turned into a contest between aircraft carriers. American carrier-launched torpedo aircraft and

bolster their courage. Though this tactic lost many pilots and aircraft, it also sank several ships. It could not, however, prevent Japan's defeat.

Aircraft everywhere

By the end of World War II, aircraft had been produced in their hundreds of thousands and were serving on every battle front. They flew over deserts, jungles, and mountains. From air transports, such as the German Junkers Ju-52, thousands of troops parachuted behind enemy lines or near key objectives. Ground-attack planes, such as the Republic P-47 Thunderbolt or Hawker Typhoon, destroyed tanks and trucks.

Warplanes today

Since the war, military aircraft have got faster, can fly farther, and now have much more powerful and accurate weaponry. Their role in war has, if anything, increased. But they have never again played as decisive a part in such an enormous war.

AMERICA'S B-1B LANCER, BUILT IN THE 1980S, IS A SUPERSONIC BOMBER THAT LOOKS AND PERFORMS LIKE A FIGHTER.

FASTER THAN SOUND

At the dawn of the "jet age" in the late 1940s, the skies echoed with the roars and screams of experimental planes. Powered by jets or rockets, their target was to travel faster than sound itself. However, test pilots found out the hard way that airplanes behave in very strange ways as they approach the speed of sound. For a while it seemed that the goal of "going supersonic" was to remain an impossible dream—a sound barrier.

Test tragedy

In September 1946, test pilot Geoffrey de Havilland took an experimental jet aircraft, the D.H. 108, into the air over England. He intended to fly it faster than any plane had gone before—faster than sound. He put the aircraft into a dive to gain speed. But as he neared the speed of sound, a violent shaking battered the airplane, as if it were a car being driven very fast over a rocky road.

Suddenly and terrifyingly, the flight controls stopped operating. However hard de Havilland pulled on the control stick, it made no difference. Accelerating out of control, the D.H. 108 broke up in the air.

Shocking speed

De Havilland was killed, but we know what he must have experienced that day because something like it happened to other pilots who lived to tell the tale. The actual

AN F/A-18 HORNET IS SHOWN AS IT BREAKS THE SOUND BARRIER. THE STRANGE CLOUD IS WATER CONDENSATION CAUSED BY THE SHOCKWAVE THE AIRPLANE CREATES AS IT SPEEDS THROUGH THE AIR.

THIS D.H. 108 WAS THE PLANE IN WHICH TEST PILOT GEOFFREY DE HAVILLAND DIED WHILE TRYING TO GO SUPERSONIC IN 1946.

speed of sound in miles or kilometers per hour varies, but it is always referred to as Mach 1. When an aircraft accelerates toward Mach 1, it runs into shock waves created by its own passage through the air.

To fliers of de Havilland's generation it seemed as if it might be impossible to fly through this "sound barrier."

Propellers meet their limit

This was a big issue in the 1940s because new jet and rocket engines had been invented that were clearly going to make aircraft much, much faster. Until then, all aircraft had been powered by propellers turned by piston engines (essentially like the engine of a car, but larger).

A very fast piston-engined aircraft, such as the World War II Mustang fighter, could reach about 450 mph (720 km/h) in level flight. This was as good as it was possible to get out of a piston engine and prop.

Jets and rockets

Jets and rockets are completely different. Anyone who has made a party balloon whiz around a room knows the basic principle—air rushing out of a hole at the back thrusts the balloon forward. Powering an aircraft this way, there was virtually no limit to the top speed—if only the sound barrier could be overcome.

How engines work

In a rocket engine, a stream of hot air is created by burning chemicals, just like when you light a firework. As long as the chemical goes on burning, the rocket zips across the sky. Space rockets carry their own supply of liquid oxygen, so they can travel in the airless emptiness of outer space.

WEIRD WORLD

THE LOUDEST SONIC BOOM EVER RECORDED CAME FROM A LOW-FLYING F-4 PHANTOM JET. THE SOUND WAS 70 TIMES AS STRONG AS THE BOOM TYPICALLY MADE BY A HIGH-FLYING CONCORDE.

Jet engines are more useful for aircraft. They take in air at the front, heat and compress it, and then push it out of a hole at the back (although it isn't always that simple). The important thing about jet engines is that they work better the faster you go and the higher you fly.

Germany's jets

The first jet aircraft engines were designed in the 1930s by Frank Whittle in Britain and Hans von Ohain in Germany.

Allied bombers. They were still experimental aircraft and scary to fly, killing almost as many of their pilots as they did of the enemy. But they were definitely the fastest machines in the sky.

Guinea pigs

After the war, solving the mystery of the sound barrier became a major priority. Nowadays, it would probably be possible to use computer models to work out what was going on. But the only way to study it back in those days was

THE X-1 FLEW FOR JUST TWO AND A HALF MINUTES ON FULL POWER.

The Nazis quickly pushed ahead with jets and rockets. During the later stages of World War II (1939–1945) Messerschmitt Me163 rocket planes and Me262 jet fighters flew in the defense of Germany against

to send a test pilot up in an aircraft and see what happened.

The Americans built an experimental rocket plane, the Bell X-1, for the purpose, and found a test pilot, Chuck Yeager, ready to risk his life

THE MESSERSCHMITT ME262 WAS THE FIRST JET FIGHTER. FLYING IN THE 1940S, IT HAD A TOP SPEED OF 541 MPH (870 KM/H), MUCH FASTER THAN ANY PISTON-ENGINED PLANE OF ITS DAY.

pushing it to the limit. Yeager called his Bell X-1 *Glamorous Glennis*, after his wife.

What a ride!

For test flights, the rocket plane was carried up to high altitude underneath a Boeing B-29 bomber. That way, the X-1 didn't need fuel for takeoff.

Yeager climbed down into the tiny cockpit, and the X-1 was dropped out of the B-29 like a bomb. Seconds later

Yeager carried out a series of these flights, gradually upping the speed, while scientists on the ground monitored him.

As the X-1 drew close to Mach 1, Yeager met the usual unnerving experiences of extreme turbulence and loss of control. But a change to the way the aircraft's controls worked resolved these problems. The turbulence was no longer so violent as Yeager crept toward the very edge of the speed of sound.

THE BELL X-1 ROCKET PLANE IS DROPPED FROM THE BELLY OF THE B-29 "MOTHERSHIP" THAT TOOK IT TO HIGH ALTITUDE.

he ignited his rocket engine and accelerated into a few minutes of high-speed flight. "God what a ride!" he later wrote. When the test was over, he switched off his engine and glided back down to land.

On October 14, 1947, during his ninth X-1 flight, Yeager was in pain after falling from a horse over the weekend and breaking two ribs. Not wishing to be grounded, he kept the injury a secret. And

53

although still forbidden by his cautious controllers to "go supersonic," he decided to go for it anyway.

People on the ground heard an ear-shattering boom. It was a noise never before heard on earth—the sonic boom that an aircraft delivers when it is

Bell X-2 exceeded Mach 3. The X-2's pilot, Milburn Apt, was the first human to travel at over 2,000 mph (3,220 km/h), but he did not live to enjoy his fame. He was killed as the X-2 flew out of control and crashed in the course of the record-breaking Mach 3 flight.

flying faster than sound. Yeager later wrote that after he passed Mach 1, "It was as smooth as a baby's bottom.

THE X-15, THE FASTEST WINGED AIRPLANE EVER, FIRED SMALL JETS TO TURN AT HIGH ALTITUDE—LIKE THE JETS THAT SPACECRAFT USE IN SPACE.

THE X-15 FLEW UP TO 67 MILES (108 KM) ABOVE EARTH.

Grandma could be sitting up there sipping lemonade." The sound barrier was broken and the way was open to higher speeds.

Faster still
Rocket aircraft launched from bombers went on to break speed records again and again. In 1953, the Douglas Skyrocket passed Mach 2 (twice the speed of sound). In 1956, the

These experiments with rocket planes reached a climax with the X-15A-2. In 1967 it reached Mach 6.72—twice the speed of a rifle bullet!

Fast fighters
Jet aircraft that took off from the ground couldn't match the X-15's speed, which was only bettered by the Space Shuttle in 1981. Soon, however, jet fighters went supersonic. The F-104

Starfighter flew at Mach 2 in level flight, and even faster in a dive—they called it "the missile with a man in it"!

These amazing speeds carried terrible risks. Many test pilots and ordinary fighter pilots died young. Parachutes were useless in aircraft moving that fast, so ejection seats were brought in.

Today the maximum speed of jet fighter aircraft is not much faster than 40 years ago. For practical purposes, Mach 2 was fast enough. Instead, jet planes have improved in other ways, from electronic control systems to more reliable engines. This has taken most of the danger out of supersonic flight.

However, while today's fighter pilots are outfitted like astronauts, the only protection Yeager had on his flights was a football helmet! The test pilots of the 1940s and 1950s were brave heroes.

But being blown out of a cockpit strapped in a seat was also extremely dangerous, even if it was better than ending up amid the twisted wreckage of an aircraft.

A MODERN JET FIGHTER PILOT SITS IN AN EJECTION SEAT. IN AN EMERGENCY, THE SEAT CAN FIRE THE PILOT FROM THE COCKPIT AT ABOUT 100 MPH (160 KM/H).

HAPPY LANDINGS!

Takeoff and landing have always been the trickiest moments in flight. It's hard enough setting a fully laden airliner down on a busy airport runway, but what if your airstrip is a rolling ship's deck or a forest clearing in a war zone? Progress in aircraft design and the use of electronic instruments have made getting up and down easier and, in some cases, quite spectacular.

Belt up

Flying is safer than driving, but as you fasten your seat belt at the start of a flight it's hard not to feel a little nervous. This, after all, is one of the two riskiest

IN 1954, THE ROLLS-ROYCE "FLYING BEDSTEAD" TRIED OUT VERTICAL TAKEOFF WITH JETS ON EACH OF ITS LEGS.

A FULL JUMBO JET NEEDS OVER 10,800 FT (3,300 M) OF RUNWAY.

parts of a flight. Luckily, airlines know how to plot the safest way into the air.

As you sit at the start of the airport runway, the crew have already worked out what speed is needed to leave the ground. This depends on the weight of the plane with its load of passengers. The more weight there is, the more speed you need. It also depends on conditions at the airport—wind strength and direction, air temperature, and so on.

A BOEING B-47 STRATOJET BOMBER OF THE 1950S BLASTS INTO THE AIR WITH THE SPECTACULAR ASSISTANCE OF ROCKETS UNDER ITS TAIL. ONCE IN FLIGHT, THE PLANE FLEW SOLELY BY JET POWER.

Assisted takeoff

The first people to have problems finding enough power to take off were the Wright brothers. The year after their famous first flights at Kitty Hawk, they tried to fly again near their home at Dayton, Ohio—and they couldn't get off the ground! This was because conditions were warmer, at a higher altitude, and

Another important factor is fuel. The longer the flight, the more fuel is needed, and so the more difficult it is for aircraft to take off. An airplane is heaviest at takeoff, when it is fully fueled. That's why runways are as long as possible—in order for airplanes to pick up enough speed to get airborne.

As soon as the airplane is cleared for takeoff, the pilot sets the engines to full power and accelerates down the runway. As the aircraft reaches the takeoff speed, the pilot pulls back on the controls. This brings the aircraft's nose up—and away it goes!

A SEA HARRIER COMES IN TO LAND ON A CARRIER. ITS ABILITY TO LAND VERTICALLY WAS ESPECIALLY USEFUL IN ROUGH WEATHER.

Rockets and piggybacks

Since the Wright *Flyer*, many airplanes have needed help of one sort or another to get airborne. Some early jet aircraft, for example, had rockets attached to their underside which blasted the plane into the air. Other aircraft have been air-launched from a "mothership"— in the same way as the Bell X-1—so they didn't have to lift off the ground under their own power at all. In the 1930s, a bizarre piggyback aircraft, the Short-Mayo composite, was tried out. This was a seaplane carried into the air by a flying boat. The seaplane "took off" in the air from the flying boat's back.

without a strong headwind. The Wrights invented a catapult to propel their *Flyer* to a high enough speed to lift off the ground. This is now called an "assisted takeoff."

Straight up

It was to avoid the need for runways that Vertical Take Off and Landing (VTOL) aircraft were invented. The first of these were "tail-sitters"— aircraft like the Convair Pogo. This stubby, propeller-driven plane took off and landed with its nose pointing straight up into the sky, turning over into horizontal flight once airborne.

Unfortunately, a tail-sitter was murderously difficult to land. The pilot had to reverse the aircraft down while lying on his back with his feet above his head. It never caught on!

The Hawker Harrier, or "jump-jet," was much more successful. Developed in the 1960s, this plane could take off and land on its wheels, as normal, but it also had jet nozzles that swiveled. They pointed downward to power the aircraft vertically into the air. Then they were angled back for normal flight. The Harrier could perform a short, rather than vertical, takeoff by setting the nozzles at an angle to fly from a short airstrip or a carrier deck.

All at sea

Taking off from an aircraft carrier creates all sorts of problems. However big the carrier, it can never provide the length of runway normally needed by a modern aircraft. The rolling and pitching of the carrier deck in a heavy

THE WINGS OF AN F-14 TOMCAT SWEEP BACK FOR SUPERSONIC FLIGHT. DURING TAKEOFF AND LANDING, THEY OPEN OUT TO PROVIDE STABILITY AT LOW SPEED.

sea doesn't help, either! The carrier can turn into the wind so that its planes always have a headwind to provide lift. But catapults are still used to "kick-start" the aircraft, blasting them to about 140 mph (225 km/h) in under four seconds from standstill.

Hooked

The one task worse than taking off from a carrier is landing. Luckily, pilots can practice this maneuver on a flight simulator before trying it for real.

To stop the aircraft in time, carriers use an arrester gear. This is a hook trailing from the tail of the aircraft which catches on a wire on the deck. It brings the plane to a dead halt within two seconds of touching down. The effect for the pilot is rather like driving into a brick wall!

Slow and steady

The key to landing an aircraft is being able to fly slowly enough. An aircraft designed to fly extremely fast may behave quite differently at low speeds. Coming in to land, an aircraft may lower flaps on its wing to change the wing shape. A shape ideal for high-speed flight is turned into a shape

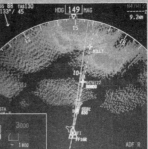

AN ARTIFICIAL HORIZON (LEFT) AND RADAR (ABOVE) IN THE COCKPIT HELP PILOTS FLY SAFELY EVEN WHEN THEY CAN'T SEE THE GROUND.

THE FLAPS ON A BOEING 747 ARE LOWERED IN READINESS FOR LANDING, ALONG WITH THE 16 MAIN WHEELS.

that gives more lift at slower speed. Jet planes may also use a parachute, known as a drag chute or drogue, that unfurls from the tail to slow them down on the runway.

Flying blind

The main hazard when landing has always been poor visibility, caused by fog or thick cloud. As long ago as 1929, American pilot Jimmy Doolittle proved that it was possible to land an aircraft "blind." His cockpit had a hood over it so he couldn't see outside. Inside he had instruments, such as an altimeter to tell him how high he was and an artificial horizon to show whether he was flying flat and level. He also had a radio to talk to a ground controller, and a radio navigation device to guide him to the airfield. Doolittle took off, flew around, and landed again without ever seeing where he was going.

Great modern gizmos

Aircrew nowadays have all the aids that Doolittle used, plus radar, onboard computers, and warning devices that, for example, tell them to "pull up" if they get too near the ground.

But pilots still very much prefer to be able to see where they're going when they come in to land. And most passengers still feel a tiny rush of relief when the wheels set down safely on the airport runway.

WEIRD WORLD
IT WAS NO FUN LANDING NAZI GERMANY'S KOMET ROCKET PLANE. THE WHEELS FELL OFF AFTER TAKEOFF, AND THE PLANE LANDED ON BELLY SKIDS. THE JARRING IMPACT OFTEN BROKE THE PILOT'S SPINE.

WHIRLYBIRDS

An aircraft that can go straight up and down, stop in mid-air, or even fly backward—that's the helicopter. It's hardly surprising that so many people—from traffic cops to rescue services, from soldiers to medics—have found it so useful. But making a helicopter that worked was even more difficult than getting a plane off the ground. It took years of experimenting and lots of brain-power to create a whirlybird that didn't just whirl and whirl!

Speed isn't everything
In the 1920s, when new air speed records were being set every year, one aircraft was advertised proudly as able to fly slower than a man could run. The aircraft was the autogiro, and it was the brainchild of a Spanish inventor, Juan de la Cierva.

This odd-looking machine had an engine and propeller at the front, like any normal plane in those days. But above the pilot's head were rotating blades of the kind we're now used to seeing on helicopters. Some autogiros had little stubby wings, but they didn't really need them. It was the rotor that created the lift to get the aircraft into the air and keep it there.

Ancient technology

The fact that a rotating wing could fly had long been known. Since medieval times, children had played with

JUAN DE LA CIERVA'S AUTOGIRO, A PLANE WITH A ROTOR, PAVED THE WAY FOR TRUE HELICOPTERS. AMATEURS STILL ENJOY FLYING AUTOGIROS TODAY.

spinning, flying toys— perhaps inspired by the flight of the winged seeds of sycamore trees.

All this meant that inventors of the Wright brothers' era knew two ways of getting air to flow over and under a wing to create lift. They could fix the wing to the aircraft and move the whole machine forward through the air—an airplane. Or they could move the wing through the air independently of the movement of the aircraft, by rotating it—a helicopter.

Up, but not away

In 1907, Frenchman Paul Cornu managed to hover above the ground for a few seconds, entering the record books for the first rotating-wing flight. But although his craft lifted briefly into the air, no one knew how to make such a machine fly around under the control of its pilot.

Autogiros were the first successful rotating-wing aircraft, but they weren't true helicopters. There was no engine driving the rotor blades. The autogiro's blades just spun freely, pushed around by the air as it flew forward with its conventional propeller. Autogiros could fly very slowly, but they couldn't hover or fly backward, as a helicopter can.

Out of control

Two big problems had to be solved before anyone could construct a helicopter that really worked.

First, it still wasn't possible to control a helicopter's flight. The second problem was that as the rotor blades spun one way, their torque (twisting power) caused the helicopter's body to spin in the opposite direction.

Beating the spin

In the 1930s, helicopter makers found two different answers to the spinning problem. German Heinrich Focke—the man usually credited with building the first true helicopter in 1937—put two big rotors on the top of his machine, rotating in opposite directions. The clockwise spin of one cancelled out the counterclockwise spin of the other. In the United States, Russian-born engineer Igor Sikorsky did it differently. He fixed a small upright rotor to the tail of his VS-300. This not only stopped the helicopter from going into a spin, but could be used to help steer the machine. Today, most helicopters use a tail rotor, Sikorsky-style, although some big helicopters have two main rotors,

A SIKORSKY S-64 SKYCRANE LIFTS A COMPLETE PREFABRICATED HOUSE. SIKORSKY IMAGINED THE SKYCRANE MIGHT CARRY COMMUTERS TO WORK IN A DANGLING "POD," BUT IT NEVER HAPPENED.

in detail how they worked. They worked out how to change the angle at which the blades cut through the air to control the amount of lift they gave, allowing the aircraft to rise, hover, or descend.

They found out that you needed a separate control to tilt the whole main rotor, which gives you the thrust to go forward and backward or turn to either side. Meanwhile, the tail rotor acts like the rudder on an airplane, helping steer the machine right or left. If this sounds complicated, it is! There's nothing simple about flying a helicopter.

Focke-style. A less common third type have little jets at the ends of their rotor blades, which also solve the spinning problem.

Blade technology

Learning how to control a helicopter so it could fly in every direction took a lot of experiments with rotor blades. Gradually, aeronautical engineers began to understand

65

6512

U.S. COAST GUARD

Versatile craft

Although helicopters are much slower than airplanes, they're amazingly useful. They can take off or land wherever there's a helicopter-sized open space, such as a building with a flat roof, or even a large front lawn. Even where they can't land, helicopters can hover and winch people up on a cable. Many shipwrecked sailors owe their lives to helicopter air–sea rescue. Helicopters have also saved the lives of thousands of accident victims by ferrying them swiftly to hospital.

THIS HELICOPTER IS DOING WHAT HELICOPTERS DO BEST, RESCUING A PERSON IN DANGER ON THE NORTHERN COAST OF CALIFORNIA.

Take the weight

By the 1960s, some helicopters were powerful enough to carry 50 people. There were plenty of roles for heavy-lift helicopters such as the Sikorsky Skycrane. They could help build skyscrapers, for instance, lowering parts for construction workers to assemble. The Russian Mil V-12 became the world's helicopter weight lifting champion in 1967 by lifting nearly 90,000 lb (40,000 kg)— the equivalent of six elephants.

Medical and military use

In war, helicopters were at first mostly used to move troops around and carry wounded soldiers from the battlefield to receive urgent medical care.

In the 1960s, however, they went on the attack. Helicopters were built with guns and rockets, capable of blasting enemy tanks or trucks. But they were still slow compared to airplanes. It's hard to make a helicopter fly even as fast as 156 mph (250 km/h).

The future

Designers dream of making a cross between a helicopter and an airplane, which could fly a lot faster. They've built "tilt-rotors"—winged airplanes with propellers that can swivel to point upward, turning into helicopter-style rotors. They've even made an experimental helicopter that turns into a jet plane. Its whirling rotor blade can be stopped in flight and locked in position to make— hey presto!—a fixed wing.

But none of these devices has yet worked especially well. Perhaps it's best in the end to accept that, for helicopters, slow is the way to go.

THE AH-64 APACHE ATTACK HELICOPTER CAN DIRECT GUNS, GUIDED MISSILES, AND ROCKETS AT AIR OR GROUND TARGETS.

INTO SPACE

I n the last 100 years, space travel has developed from science fiction into everyday reality. We live in a world where space tourists have paid for trips into orbit and numerous satellites—uncrewed spacecraft—circle Earth, helping us predict the weather or navigate when driving cars. But the most fascinating goal remains sending craft with humans on board to explore deep space—the final frontier.

To boldly go
Imagine being the first person to travel to outer space. You are squashed inside a small, round capsule perched on top of a massive rocket. The rocket engines ignite with a roar and you are lifted up into the sky, the continents and oceans passing below you like the pages of a giant atlas.

The first human in space
That was the experience of Soviet cosmonaut Yuri Gagarin, who carried out the first space

ONLY 12 PEOPLE HAVE WALKED ON THE SURFACE OF THE MOON.

are lifted up into the sky, accelerating so fast that you are pinned back in your seat as if by great weights.

After a few minutes, though, the rocket booster falls away and you are in orbit around Earth. You are weightless, alone in space, witnessing a spectacle that no one has ever seen before—

flight on April 12, 1961, circling the globe in just over an hour and a half. He had achieved a feat that had long seemed impossible. Space travel had been seen as the stuff of science fiction, not science fact.

THE SOVIET ROCKET VOSTOK 1 LIFTS OFF TO SEND YURI GAGARIN (INSET) ON THE FIRST HUMAN FLIGHT INTO OUTER SPACE.

Defying gravity

In some ways, however, space flight posed a simpler problem to inventors than airplane flight. In the 1800s, French fantasy novelist Jules Verne had the idea of sending someone into space as a human cannon-ball, fired from a huge gun. This wasn't totally ridiculous.

What holds you to the ground is the pull of Earth's gravity on your body. If you were propelled by a sufficient upward force to overcome the pull of gravity, you would end up in space.

Impossible speed

During the early 20th century, scientists such as the American Robert Goddard showed how,

in theory, you could get enough oomph—from a liquid-fueled rocket, rather than a gun. Building such a rocket posed a challenge. The speed an astronaut would need to reach to break free of Earth's gravity was a staggering 25,000 mph (40,000 km/h).

Missile technology

The eventual breakthrough in rocket development came at a terrible cost. During World War II, governments spent vast sums of money on creating rockets for use as weapons.

The first really effective rockets were the Nazis' V-2 missiles, developed by Wernher von Braun in Germany during World War II. After the war, building on the Nazis' lead, the United States and its Cold War enemy the Soviet Union

MEN ARE SHOT TO THE LUNAR SURFACE IN A GIANT SHELL IN *A TRIP TO THE MOON*, A 1902 FILM BY GEORGE MELIES.

THE ANCESTOR OF ALL SPACE ROCKETS WAS THE V-2, BUILT AS A WEAPON BY THE NAZIS DURING WORLD WAR II.

developed ever more powerful rockets, designed to attack distant cities. Scientists knew that the same rockets could be used to send objects into space.

Sputnik 1

In 1957, the Soviet Union launched *Sputnik 1*, the first satellite, into Earth's orbit. *Sputnik 1* was tiny—about twice the size of a soccer ball—and its only function was to circle the space, the dog Laika. Sadly, Laika was not to return.

The race is on

After *Sputnik*, the race was on between the Soviet Union and the United States to put a human into space.

Both countries took fighter pilots and trained them to be astronauts (the American word) or cosmonauts (Soviet-style). They designed pressurized spacesuits and cabins to protect the space traveler outside Earth's atmosphere, and heat shields to stop the spacecraft from burning up as it reentered the atmosphere at high speed.

SPACE VOYAGERS HAVE INCLUDED FROGS, CHIMPS, AND INSECTS.

globe emitting a regular "beep" from its radio transmitters. But it marked the beginning of the space age.

Later in 1957, the Soviets put the first living creature into

THE DOG LAIKA WAITS TO BECOME THE FIRST EARTH CREATURE TO ENTER SPACE.

Before Gagarin's flight no one knew if it would all work—but it did, and for a while he was the world's most famous human.

Kennedy's great goal

Americans were shocked that the Soviets had beaten them into space. The United States was never far behind—Alan Shepard became the first American in space in May 1961, less than a month after Gagarin.

But being second was not the American way, and US president John F. Kennedy committed his nation to the goal of putting a man on the moon before the decade's end. It seemed an impossible challenge. To reach the moon would need a more powerful rocket than to lift someone into orbit. Astronauts would also have to live in space for long periods. In a series of space missions in 1965 and 1966, called the *Gemini* program, US astronauts learned how to maneuver in space, dock one craft with another, and carry out "space walks."

ED WHITE MAKES THE FIRST SPACE WALK BY AN AMERICAN ASTRONAUT ON JUNE 3, 1965. IN HIS RIGHT HAND IS A "GUN" HE COULD FIRE TO MANEUVER IN SPACE.

The Soviets struggled to keep up. In 1964, they notched up another first— the first craft to carry a crew of three into space. But they had to send the threesome up without spacesuits, since their capsule was too small!

Big blaster

By the end of 1967, the Americans had their moon rocket. At 3,307 tons (3,000 metric tons) the Saturn V launcher was the heaviest object ever to fly. It was also the most powerful flying machine ever built. When it took off from Cape Canaveral, it shook the surrounding land like an earthquake. The Saturn V was built in three sections, each with its own set of rockets and fuel supply. As each section was used up, it fell away into space, and the next section took over. On top of the rocket were a Command and Service Module (CSM) in which the astronauts would enter the moon's orbit, and a Lunar Module (LM) to descend to the moon's surface.

ON LATER MOON MISSIONS, ASTRONAUTS TRAVELED IN THE LUNAR ROVER (SEEN HERE PARKED BESIDE THE LUNAR MODULE).

At Christmas in 1968, three astronauts orbited the moon on board *Apollo 8*, sending back stunning images of Earth.

Moonshot

The moon landing came on July 20, 1969. Astronauts Neil Armstrong and Buzz Aldrin descended to the moon's surface in the LM from the *Apollo 11* craft, while Michael Collins stayed in lunar orbit aboard its CSM. Watched by millions of people on TV, Armstrong and Aldrin planted an American flag and collected rock samples, before heading back to Earth. The US went on to land another 10 men on the moon before terminating the program in 1972.

Reusable spacecraft

The moon landings were a hard act to follow. However, the US space agency NASA went on to produce something just as remarkable in its way: the Space Shuttle.

From the start of the space age, people had dreamed of an airplane that flew into space and back. The Shuttle was not quite a "space plane," as it needed booster rockets to lift it into space. Still, it was truly reusable, gliding down to an airstrip after a space mission. Shuttle duties would include launching satellites and visiting space stations. The Shuttle stayed in service for 30 years. Two Shuttles were lost in tragic accidents, *Challenger* exploding after launch in 1986 and *Columbia* breaking up as it reentered Earth's atmosphere in 2003. Shuttle missions ended in 2011.

BLAST-OFF! TWO ROCKET BOOSTERS, FIXED TO A HUGE BROWN FUEL TANK, LAUNCH THE SPACE SHUTTLE INTO THE SKY.

Living in space

Space stations are crewed spacecraft that orbit Earth and have made possible a permanent human presence in space. The Soviet Union launched the first space station, *Salyut 1*, in 1971. This was followed by *Mir*, launched in 1985, which stayed in orbit for 16 years. The International Space Station (ISS), created by teams from 16 nations, has been continuously occupied since the year 2000.

Life in space isn't easy. Everything floats away in the gravity-free environment, even water. Space-station dwellers shower inside a bag to keep the liquid in. They even sleep in sleeping bags tied to a wall. Keeping a sense of daily routine is hard because the sun rises and sets 16 times every 24 hours. However, humans have survived in these conditions, showing that long-term habitation is possible. One cosmonaut, Valeri Polyakov, lived on board *Mir* for 14 months in a row in 1994–1995.

The United States and Russia have long ceased to dominate space exploration. China carried out its first crewed space flight in 2003 and plans to land a person on the moon, and India, too, has an ambitious space program.

Space tourism

In April 2001, American businessman Dennis Tito became the first space tourist, paying $20 million for a trip to the ISS. Since then, several inventors have joined the race to develop a vehicle that would carry passengers into orbit on the trip of a lifetime. Safety issues have made progress slow, but this has not deterred space enthusiasts who continue to snap up tickets on potential flights to the moon or even to Mars. Clearly, the history of space flight has only just begun.

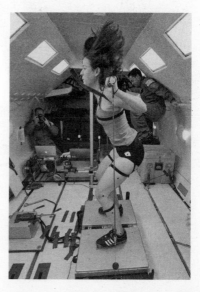

ASTRONAUTS TRAIN AT OPERATING IN A GRAVITY-FREE ENVIRONMENT. THIS ASTRONAUT TRAINS IN A LARGE PLANE THAT CREATES WEIGHTLESS CONDITIONS BY FALLING STEEPLY—A BIT LIKE A CARNIVAL RIDE.

EXTREME AIRCRAFT

A ircraft powered by the sun, aircraft pedaled like bicycles, aircraft that fly at three times the speed of sound, aircraft that cruise at the speed a person can run—in their dazzling diversity, flying machines are wonders of the modern world. Over a century after the Wright brothers, inventors and adventurers continue to push back the frontiers of flight.

Sky's the limit

With modern technical know-how, engine power, and new materials, there seems almost no limit to what a flying machine can be made to do.

Take the Lockheed SR-71 Blackbird. This aircraft was designed as a spy plane, meant to travel so high and fast over enemy territory that no fighter aircraft or missile could shoot it down.

Built in the 1960s, the Blackbird looks impressive, with its sinister black paint (to help evade radar) and bladelike body. But its performance is even

THE SR-71 SERVED AS AN AMERICAN SPY PLANE UNTIL THE 1990S. ITS POWERFUL CAMERAS COULD SPOT A GOLF BALL FROM 15 MILES (24 KM) UP.

more amazing than its looks. The Blackbird can cruise at altitudes of over 16 miles (25.5 km) at Mach 3—over 2,000 mph (3,200 km/h)!

THE ANGLO-FRENCH CONCORDE, THE WORLD'S ONLY SUPERSONIC AIRLINER, COULD FLY A MILE IN LESS THAN THREE SECONDS.

Hot stuff

Flying at such speed makes the plane's skin very hot, through friction (rubbing) with the air.

The Blackbird is mostly made of titanium alloy, a special material that is light- and heat-resistant. Even so, when the aircraft lands after a mission its metal nose is often wrinkled by the heat. It has to be flattened out by ground staff using a blowtorch, much as you might iron a shirt!

Surprisingly, a speeding Blackbird is no gas-guzzler. When it flies flat out, air rushes through its engines so fast that the aircraft is propelled forward with hardly any need for the engines to burn fuel. This plane can virtually run on air.

Out of this world

Piloting an SR-71 Blackbird is an unforgettable experience. You travel faster than Earth's rotation, so if you fly westward at top speed, you see the sun rise in the west, instead of setting there. If you fly eastward, adding the speed of Earth's rotation to your own, you pass from day into night quite suddenly, like flying into a black curtain.

77

From the 1970s, the experience of supersonic flight was opened up to anyone with enough cash to buy a ticket on the Concorde airliner. Concorde flew at twice the speed of sound, yet its passengers sat comfortably sipping cups of coffee. The only way you could tell you were moving fast was to touch the windows, which were hot from friction with the air. Concorde was retired from service in 2003.

What a blast!

For the real buzz of speed, nothing beats the experience of flying a modern jet-fighter. A plane such as the F-15 can rise like a rocket to the height of Mount Everest (29,020 ft/8,848 m) in under a minute from takeoff.

When the pilot ignites the afterburner, spraying fuel into the hot engine exhaust to go supersonic, the explosive kick is awesome! Or try skimming just above treetop height at about the speed of sound, the aircraft bucking as the autopilot makes it follow every dip and bump of the ground ….

High stress

Fighter pilots wear a lot of special gear, and they need it because their aircraft can survive more strain than they can. In the days of aircraft made of canvas and wood, the risk of turning too tight and fast was

WEIRD WORLD
MANY EXPERTS BELIEVE THAT FUTURE AIR WARS WILL BE FOUGHT WITHOUT PILOTS, AS FIGHTERS FLOWN BY COMPUTERS TAKE ONE ANOTHER ON IN UNCREWED COMBAT.

that your aircraft might break up. In a modern fighter, the risk is that the pilot might lose consciousness— or worse.

An aircraft such as the F-35 fighter is capable of fast, tight turns that would usually make a human pass out in seconds. Pilots fight back by donning "g-suits," like a pair of very tight shorts. These squeeze their lower body, forcing blood up to their chest and brain and helping raise their resistance.

Fighter pilots also wear helmets, oxygen masks, and sometimes also pressurized suits, like those worn by astronauts. It's a long way from the days when fliers liked to feel the wind in their hair!

The power of thought

Without computer wizardry, jet fighters would be unflyable. Everything happens too fast and is too complicated for any human to manage.

But even with the help of computers and touch-of-a-button "fly-by-wire" controls, fighter pilots find it ever more difficult to cope. An idea being seriously explored is to link the aircraft controls directly to the pilot's brain waves, so that the pilot simply "thinks" commands in order to fly the plane.

tons (600 metric tons) at takeoff. How is it possible to move such massive weights around the sky, supported by thin air?

The simple answer is engine power. The Wright brothers believed that their invention would never work for large-scale

THE AIRBUS BELUGA, ONE OF THE BIGGEST OF ALL AIR TRANSPORTERS, CARRIES AIRLINER PARTS FROM ONE FACTORY TO ANOTHER.

Giants of the airways

If some aircraft are remarkably fast, others stand out for their size. When a fully laden Boeing 747-400 jumbo jet lifts off, there's about 441 tons (400 metric tons) of aircraft, fuel, passengers, crew, and luggage heading into the sky. The Airbus 380, which made its debut at world airports in 2007, dwarfs the 747. The largest airliner ever built, with a huge double-decker interior, it typically seats 525 passengers, but could carry as many as 850. The A380 weighs almost 661

airliners—they thought aircraft would always be light, flimsy "kites."

The piston engines available in the Wrights' day were no more powerful than those in a small car or a motorcycle. The engines of a jumbo jet are closer in scale to the engines that drive big ships. Given powerful enough engines, and using the same principles of flight that worked for the Wright brothers in 1903, plane designers can make almost any size aircraft fly.

Ghost planes

Today, you can also make an aircraft almost any shape you like. When designers in the 1980s were asked to create "stealth" planes, invisible to radar, they came up with some of the oddest-looking craft ever to fly. The F-117 stealth fighter was all strange angles, so menacing in its black paint that it was nicknamed the "Bat Plane."

The B-2 stealth bomber, on the other hand, is all wavy curves, a "flying wing" with no fuselage at all.

WEIRD WORLD

THE COCKPIT GLASS ON STEALTH AIRCRAFT IS PAINTED WITH GOLD, WHICH BLOCKS RADAR PULSES. OTHERWISE ENEMY RADAR WOULD SPOT THE BACK OF A PILOT'S METAL HELMET THROUGH THEIR HEAD!

The point of these shapes is to confuse enemy radar, and it works. Stealth planes can steal through air defenses at night, invisible as ghosts. They're not an ideal shape for flying, but that doesn't matter. Aircraft designers joke that engines and electronic control systems are now so good that, if they wanted, they could fly the Statue of Liberty.

TO AN ENEMY'S RADAR THE STEALTH FIGHTER LOOKED NO LARGER THAN A SPARROW, THANKS TO ITS BIZARRE BODY SHAPE AND COLOR.

Going the distance

However advanced aircraft have become, fliers always seem to find new challenges. In 1986, for example, Americans Dick Rutan and Jeana Yeager became the first people to fly nonstop around the world without in-flight refueling—something none of the latest airliners or military planes could do.

Rutan and Yeager's propeller-driven plane, *Voyager*, was purpose-built from super-light materials. It flew for 26,382 miles (42,212 km) on the fuel it had at takeoff.

The entire journey took nine days because *Voyager* traveled no faster than 110 mph (176 km/h)—any faster and it would have used up too much fuel. The pair spent those nine days and nights in a cockpit less than 2 ft (60 cm) wide. Luckily, they were good friends!

Pedal power

Even the dream of human-powered flight has at last been fulfilled. Scientists knew that humans could never fly by flapping their arms. But nobody said it couldn't be done by pedaling with your legs.

In 1977, a team in California built the *Gossamer Condor*, an aircraft that weighed next to nothing and had a propeller turned by pedals

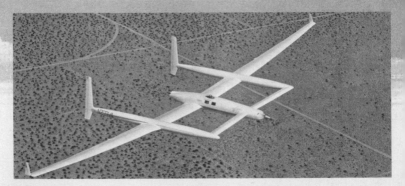

like those on a bicycle. Cyclist Bryan Allen piloted the *Condor* around a figure-of-eight course 1.5 miles (2.4 km) long.

This first human-powered flight has since been followed by many more. In 1988, for

VOYAGER FLEW NONSTOP AROUND THE WORLD IN 1986. THOUGH LIGHT, IT HAD A LONGER WING THAN MOST AIRLINERS.

GOSSAMER PENGUIN

DUPONT

Full circle

The same spirit of record-breaking and adventure-seeking brought a surprise comeback for ballooning, the earliest form of human flight.

In the 1990s, an epic contest developed to see who would be the first to fly a balloon around the world. Using the jet stream, the strong winds that blow at very high altitude around the globe, balloonists were able to travel at speeds of well over 100 mph (160 km/h).

In March 1999, Bertrand Piccard and Brian Jones finally made it around the world in their balloon *Breitling Orbiter 3*, taking just under 20 days.

instance, Greek cyclist Kanellos Kanellopoulos pedaled 74 miles (118 km) over the Aegean Sea between the islands of Crete and Santorini—the route said to have been taken by the mythical Daedalus. Pedal-powered craft aren't exactly useful, but who could resist proving it could be done?

Going green

In the early 21st century, inventors faced a new challenge as pressure mounted to make flight "green." Was it possible to create aircraft that would cause no damage to the environment?

One answer lay in covering an aircraft with solar panels that transformed sunlight into electricity, powering the plane with "clean" energy. In 2015–2016 the solar-powered aircraft *Solar Impulse 2* flew around the world, proving an aircraft could cross oceans and continents without using polluting fuel.

THE NORTHROP GRUMMAN BAT DRONE CARRIES OUT RECONNAISSANCE MISSIONS FOR THE US ARMED FORCES. IT CAN STAY IN THE AIR FOR UP TO 18 HOURS.

Pioneering spirit

One area that saw a surge of development and interest in the 21st century was the use of drones—aircraft that don't have pilots on board. However, no matter how useful these uncrewed aircraft are, the human urge to fly is never going to die. The spirit of aviation pioneers is still very much alive.

In 2012, skydiver Felix Baumgartner broke the sound barrier while falling to Earth almost from the edge of space. Then, in 2019, French inventor Franky Zapata flew across the English Channel standing on a jet-powered hoverboard. Every summer ordinary people leap off cliffs in hang gliders. No one will ever persuade humans to leave the skies to the birds.

THE *ZAPATA FLYBOARD* IS POWERED BY KEROSENE-FUELED COMBUSTION TURBINES, AND CAN ACHIEVE SPEEDS OF UP TO 110 MPH (177 KM/H).

REFERENCE
SECTION

Whether you've finished reading
Flight, or are turning to this section
first, you'll find the information
on the next eight pages really
helpful. Here are all the aviation
facts and figures, background details,
and unfamiliar words that you might
need. You'll also find a useful list
of websites—so whether you want
to surf the internet or look for flight
facts, these pages should turn you
from an enthusiast into an expert.

HISTORIC MOMENTS IN FLIGHT

November 21, 1783
The Marquis d'Arlandes and Pilâtre
de Rozier make the first air journey
in a Montgolfier balloon.

1809–1810
Sir George Cayley publishes *On
Aerial Navigation*, setting out the basic
principles of heavier-than-air flight.

1852
Henri Giffard flies a steam-powered
balloon, the first powered aircraft.

1890
Clément Ader's steam-powered
airplane, the *Éole*, briefly lifts
from the ground.

1900
The Wright brothers begin glider
flights at Kitty Hawk, North
Carolina. Count Zeppelin builds
his first airship.

December 17, 1903
The Wrights achieve the first
powered, sustained, controlled,
heavier-than-air flight at Kill Devil
Hills, near Kitty Hawk.

1904–1905
The Wrights continue their flight
experiments, staying airborne for
over half an hour at a time.

November 13, 1907
Paul Cornu achieves the first lift-off
in a primitive helicopter.

January 1908
In Paris, Henri Farman flies a 0.6-mile
(1-km) circuit in a Voisin biplane.
The French hail this as the first true,
heavier-than-air flight.

August 1908
Wilbur Wright flies in France. The
Wright brothers are recognized as
having been the first to fly.

July 25, 1909
Louis Blériot is the first person
to fly a plane across the
English Channel.

August 1909
The world's first air show is held
in Reims, France.

October 22, 1909
Raymonde de Laroche becomes the
first woman to pilot an airplane.

1910
Zeppelin airships begin the world's
first air passenger service.

1911
Cal Rodgers flies across the United
States from coast to coast. Aircraft
are used for the first time in war,
by Italy against Turkey in Libya.

1914
Igor Sikorsky flies his four-engined
aircraft *Ilya Muromets* a distance of
1,625 miles (2,600 km).

1915
In World War I, the first dogfights
take place between rival fighter
aircraft. Zeppelin airships conduct
the first air raids on London.

April 21, 1918
German air ace Manfred "Red Baron"
von Richthofen is killed.

1919
The first regular airline services
start up in Europe.

June 14–15 ,1919
John Alcock and Arthur Brown
make the first nonstop flight across
the Atlantic Ocean.

1921
American air commander Billy
Mitchell stages the first sinking
of a battleship by an aircraft.

1926
American scientist Robert Goddard makes the first liquid-fueled rocket.

May 20–21, 1927
Charles Lindbergh flies solo from New York to Paris.

1929
The airship *Graf Zeppelin* flies around the world in 21 days.

May 5–24, 1930
Pilot Amy Johnson flies solo from England to Australia.

1932
Amelia Earhart is the first woman to fly solo across the Atlantic Ocean.

1936
The Douglas DC-3 airliner appears. The Focke-Achgelis FW 61, the first practical helicopter, flies.

May 6, 1937
The airship *Hindenburg* is destroyed by fire at Lakehurst, New Jersey.

August 27 ,1939
Flight of the first jet-powered aircraft, the Heinkel He 178.

August–October 1940
The Battle of Britain—the first battle fought in the air alone—takes place.

December 7 ,1941
Japanese carrier-borne aircraft bomb the US fleet at Pearl Harbor.

1944
The first jet aircraft fly in warfare. The Germans launch V-2 rockets against London and Antwerp.

October 14, 1947
Chuck Yeager breaks the sound barrier (Mach 1) in the Bell X-1 rocket plane.

1952
The world's first jet airliner, the De Havilland Comet, enters service.

November 1953
Scott Crossfield passes Mach 2 in the Douglas Skyrocket.

1958
The Boeing 707 jet airliner enters commercial service.

April 12, 1961
Soviet cosmonaut Yuri Gagarin becomes the first person in space.

1965
American and Soviet crews make the first space walks.

1966
The Harrier V/STOL aircraft is successfully flown.

July 20 ,1969
Neil Armstrong becomes the first person to walk on the moon.

1970
The Boeing 747, the first jumbo jet, enters commercial service.

1976
The supersonic airliner Concorde enters service.

August 23 ,1977
Bryan Allen makes a human-powered flight in the *Gossamer Condor*.

April 1981
The Space Shuttle enters service.

December 1985
Dick Rutan and Jeana Yeager fly around the world nonstop without refueling in their airplane *Voyager*.

March 1999
Bertrand Piccard and Brian Jones fly around the world nonstop in the balloon *Breitling Orbiter* 3.

April 2001
American businessman Dennis Tito becomes the first paying space tourist.

2007
The Airbus 380, the world's largest airliner, enters service.

July 2016
The sun-powered *Solar Impulse* 2 completes an around-the-world flight.

HEROES OF AVIATION

Clément Ader (1841–1925)
French engineer Ader made a steam-powered airplane that briefly lifted off the ground in 1890. When he built a more ambitious machine for the French Army, however, it would not fly at all.

Louis Blériot (1872–1936)
French businessman Blériot built the monoplane in which he crossed the English Channel in 1909. He later gave up flying as too dangerous, and manufactured airplanes instead.

Sir George Cayley (1773–1857)
Cayley carried out experiments with models and full-size gliders, and wrote a scientific description of the basics of heavier-than-air flight.

Jacqueline Cochran (1906–1980)
Known as the "Speed Queen," American pilot Jackie Cochran first became famous as an air racer in the 1930s. Flying jet aircraft in the 1950s, she was the first woman to break the sound barrier.

Bessie Coleman (1896–1926)
US flying schools would not accept an African American woman, so Coleman learned to fly in France. "Queen Bess" later became a famous stunt flier.

Glenn Curtiss (1878–1930)
In 1909, this American former bike racer set a world air speed record of 47 mph (75 km/h) in France. He later made seaplanes and flying boats.

James Doolittle (1896–1993)
A stunt flier and racing pilot in the 1920s, Doolittle's feats included making the first "blind" flight and winning the 1932 Thompson Trophy in a Gee Bee Racer. In 1942, he led a famous raid on Japan by carrier-launched B-25 bombers .

Amelia Earhart (1898–1937)
Earhart was the first woman to fly across the Atlantic, as a passenger, in 1927, and the first woman to pilot a plane across the Atlantic in 1932. She disappeared over the Pacific while trying to fly around the world.

Henri Farman (1874–1958)
Paris-born Farman made a number of record-breaking flights in 1908–1909. He was the first person to fly a plane from one town to another. With his brother, Maurice, he became one of France's top aircraft manufacturers.

Howard Hughes (1905–1976)
An eccentric millionaire who also made movies, Hughes became a leading pilot in the 1930s, setting a number of records. He built the largest airplane ever, the Hercules "Spruce Goose" flying boat, but it flew only once, in 1947.

Amy Johnson (1903–1941)
In 1930, British amateur pilot Johnson bought herself a Gypsy Moth aircraft and flew it solo to Australia. She made many more record-breaking flights but disappeared piloting a plane in World War II.

Charles Kingsford Smith (1897–1935)
The most famous Australian flier, in 1928 Kingsford Smith was first to fly across the Pacific from the US to Australia. In 1929, he founded Australian National Airways. He disappeared near Burma (Myanmar) attempting an England–Australia flight.

Otto Lilienthal (1848–1896)
German engineer Lilienthal's trials with early gliders and his writings on bird flight had a profound influence on the Wright brothers. He was killed in a glider crash.

Charles Lindbergh (1902–1974)
Lindbergh was a barnstormer and an air-mail pilot before winning fame for flying solo from New York to Paris in 1927. He made other pioneering flights, and promoted aviation in his native United States.

R. J. Mitchell (1895–1937)
English aircraft designer Reginald Mitchell worked for the Supermarine company. He designed the Spitfire fighter, as well as the seaplanes that won the Schneider Trophy.

Charles Nungesser (1892–1927)
Nungesser, a French air ace during World War I, scored 43 kills despite being injured in crashes. In 1927, he attempted, with François Coli, to fly from Paris to New York. They disappeared without trace.

Baron Manfred von Richthofen (1892–1918)
Known as the Red Baron, this German cavalry officer took up flying in 1915. Fighting in World War I, he scored 80 kills, leading other fighter pilots in "Richthofen's Flying Circus." He was shot down and killed in the last year of the war.

Igor Sikorsky (1889–1972)
Sikorsky began designing aircraft in Russia before 1914, including the multi-engined *Ilya Muromets*. Moving to the United States, he built flying boats before creating the pioneering VS-300 helicopter in 1939.

Sir Frank Whittle (1907–1996)
In the early 1930s, Whittle, a Royal Air Force pilot, designed a turbojet air engine in his spare time. The first British jet with a Whittle engine flew in 1941.

Orville and Wilbur Wright (1871–1948 and 1867–1912)
Born in Dayton, Ohio, the Wright brothers made bicycles before taking up flight experiments in 1900. By 1905 they had an airplane capable of substantial flights, demonstrating it in public in 1908. After 1910 they played little part in aviation.

Chuck Yeager (1923–)
Yeager joined the US Army Air Corps and flew Mustang fighters against Germany in World War II. After the war he became a test pilot, passing Mach 1 in 1947 and breaking other speed records into the 1950s.

Count Ferdinand von Zeppelin (1838–1917)
German aristocrat Count Zeppelin was more than 60 years old when his first airship, LZ1, flew in July 1900. He went on to become a national hero, living to see zeppelins used as bombers in World War I.

FLIGHT GLOSSARY

Afterburner
Device that sprays fuel into the rear nozzle of a jet engine where it ignites to create extra thrust.

Airplane
Heavier-than-air powered flying machine with a fixed wing or wings.

Airship
Powered, lighter-than-air aircraft.

Altimeter
Cockpit instrument that shows an aircraft's height above the ground.

Artificial horizon
Cockpit instrument that shows whether the plane is in level flight.

Assisted takeoff
Takeoff with the use of power from, for example, rockets or a catapult.

Autogiro
Aircraft with both a propeller and a helicopter-style rotor.

Automatic pilot (or autopilot)
Device that takes over some of an aircraft's controls from the pilot.

Barnstormer
Flier in the United States in the 1920s and 1930s who earned a living performing death-defying stunts.

Biplane
Airplane with two wings, one above the other.

Dirigible
Another word for an airship.

Drag
Force that holds back an aircraft as it pushes forward through the air.

Fuselage
The body of an airplane, to which the wings and tail are attached.

Flying boat
Plane that can operate from water.

Glider
Heavier-than-air aircraft without an engine. It flies by riding on thermals (rising warm air flows).

Jet engine
Engine that creates forward motion by forcing hot gas out of a nozzle at the back.

Jumbo jet
Large, wide-bodied airliner such as the Boeing 747.

Lift
The upward force that helps a plane fly, generated by air passing more quickly over the wing than under it.

Mach number
Number used to show aircraft speed relative to the speed of sound—Mach 1 is the speed of sound.

Monoplane
Airplane with one wing.

Piston engine
Internal-combustion engine that, on an aircraft, powers a propeller.

Pitch
Movement of an aircraft's nose up or down (see *roll* and *yaw*).

Pressurized cabin
Aircraft interior that is kept at a comfortable air pressure even at high altitude, where air pressure is low.

Radar
Device for detecting distant objects by bouncing radio pulses off them.

Retractable undercarriage
Wheels that can be pulled up into an aircraft's fuselage or wings after takeoff and lowered again for landing.

Roll
Tilting movement of an aircraft in which one wingtip

rises and the other falls (see
pitch and *yaw*).

Rotating-wing craft
Helicopter or autogiro.

Seaplane
Airplane with floats for taking off
from and landing on the water.

Sound barrier
The impossibility of reaching the
speed of sound in an aircraft that is
not designed for supersonic flight.

Stall
An aircraft is said to stall when low
air flow over the wings (at very
low speed) causes the plane to drop.

Stealth
Military technology that reduces an
aircraft's visibility on a radar screen.

Stratosphere
One of the higher layers of Earth's
atmosphere.

Supersonic
Faster than the speed of sound.

Thrust
Force that drives an aircraft
or rocket.

Turbulence
Violent movement of air currents.

VTOL
Stands for Vertical Take Off and
Landing, a term for planes such as
the Hawker Harrier which need
no runway.

Wind-tunnel
Device for testing aircraft designs
by simulating the effects of flying.

Yaw
Movement of an aircraft's nose
to right or left (see *pitch* and *roll*).

Zeppelin
German airship, especially one built
by Count von Zeppelin's company.

GREAT AIRCRAFT

Wright *Flyer*
The first airplane to achieve
sustained, powered flight, the
Wright 1903 *Flyer* made only
four flights, all on the same day.
A biplane with a 12-hp engine,
it reached 30 mph (48 km/h)
over a maximum distance of
850 ft (260 m).

Bleriot XI
The monoplane in which Blériot
crossed the English Channel in 1909
became one of the best-selling
aircraft of its day. The original
version, with a 25-hp engine, had a
top speed of 36 mph (58 km/h). Later
models fitted with 60-hp Gnome
rotary engines were faster.

Fokker D7
A German biplane single-seat
fighter from late in World War I,
the Fokker D7 had a 185-hp
engine and a top speed of 117 mph
(187 km/h).

Ford Trimotor
This corrugated-metal monoplane
airliner was introduced in 1926.
With three 220-hp engines, the
"Tin Goose" carried 15 passengers
at up to 125 mph (200 km/h).

Douglas DC-3
The all-metal DC-3 entered service
in 1936. It had two 1,200-hp engines
and carried up to 21 passengers at
185 mph (296 km/h), crossing the

United States with two or three stops. By 1939, the DC-3 carried 90 percent of the world's airline traffic.

Supermarine Spitfire
First flown in 1936, the Spitfire was one of a new generation of all-metal, single-seat monoplane fighters. With a 1,470-hp engine it could fly at over 350 mph (560 km/h) at altitudes of up to 36,500 ft (11,130 m).

B-17 Flying Fortress
The Americans used the Boeing B-17 to bomb Germany in World War II. It had a 4,000-lb (1,816-kg) bomb capacity and 10 crew, and carried up to 13 machine-guns in defense.

North American P-51 Mustang
One of the best late–World War II single-seat fighters, the Mustang reached 450 mph (720 km/h) and flew over 2,000 miles (3,200 km) without refueling.

Messerschmitt Me 262
The first jet fighter, used by the Nazis in 1944–1945, the Me 262 had two 1,984-lb (8.8-kN) thrust turbojet engines. It could reach speeds of 540 mph (860 km/h).

North American F-86 Sabre
Entering service with the US Air Force in 1948, the Sabre single-seat jet fighter saw action in the Korean War (1950–1953).

Boeing B-52 Stratofortress
The B-52 was introduced in 1955. A giant jet bomber capable of delivering nuclear weapons, the Stratofortress was the mainstay

of America's Strategic Air Command during the post-war Cold War era. It was still in service in 2020.

Boeing 707
The Boeing 707 was the first truly successful jet airliner. Introduced in 1958, it stayed in production until 1977. In the version with four 19,000-lb (85-kN) thrust turbofan engines the 707 carried 147 passengers a maximum of 5,000 miles (8,000 km) at about 600 mph (970 km/h).

MiG-21
The Soviet MiG-21 single-seat fighter flies at up to 1,390 mph (2,220 km/h). Introduced in 1959, it was still in service in 2020 with 19 countries.

Lockheed SR-71 Blackbird
First flown in 1962, this spy plane was the world's fastest winged jet aircraft, reaching 2,250 mph (3,600 km/h) and operating at a maximum altitude of 100,000 ft (30,500 m). The Blackbird was retired in 1998.

Boeing 747
Introduced in 1969, the 747 was the first jumbo jet. It can carry 420 passengers about 6,800 miles (10,880 km) at 590 mph (940 km/h).

Aerospatiale/BAE Concorde
A supersonic airliner, Concorde could carry 128 passengers at up to 1,354 mph (2,166 km/h). It was in commercial service from 1976 to 2003.

Airbus A380
The world's largest passenger airliner, the A380 entered service in 2007. It can carry more than 500 passengers over almost 9,000 miles (15,000 km).

FLIGHT WEBSITES

There are many websites detailing the history of flight. Some introduce the collections of aviation museums around the world.

airandspace.si.edu/
The Smithsonian National Air and Space Museum, in Washington, D.C., is home to a spectacular collection of historic aircraft, as well as rockets and other spacecraft.

airships.net
A rich collection of information and images relating to the golden age of airship travel.

aviation-history.com
This online museum provides an absorbing collection of video clips, articles, and images ranging over the whole history of flight.

centennialofflight.net
Useful information on the Wright brothers and the history of flight in general, provided by the US Centennial of Flight Commission.

iwm.org.uk/iwm-duxford/about
This website covers the Imperial War Museum's collection at RAF Duxford, UK. The airfield itself hosts regular air shows.

museumofflight.org
Among the collection at the Seattle Museum of Flight in Washington state are historic aircraft from the Boeing Company. They include the "Flying White House," the air transport of former US presidents.

nasa.gov
A mass of fascinating material is available at the official NASA website, especially on the subject of space exploration.

nationalmuseum.af.mil/
The US Air Force Museum in Dayton, Ohio, has a huge array of military aircraft, and is home to the National Aviation Hall of Fame.

rafmuseum.org.uk
The RAF Museum's collection at Hendon, London, UK, has more than 130 aircraft, including many from World War I and World War II.

INDEX

ACKNOWLEDGMENTS

The publisher would like to thank the following people for their help with making the book:
Virien Chopra, Sukriti Kapoor, and Sai Prasanna for editorial assistance; Rakesh Kumar, Priyanka Sharma, and Saloni Singh for the jacket; Chris Bernstein for the index; MSgt William Ackerman and Maj. Christopher Pirkl, 48th Fighter Wing, USAF; and Katherine Boyce, RAF Museum, Hendon.